DESIGNING
—WITH—
COLOUR

DESIGNING
— WITH —
COLOUR

**How the language of colour works and how
to manipulate it in your graphic designs**

A QUARTO BOOK

Copyright © 1991 Quarto Publishing plc

Published by B.T. Batsford Ltd
4 Fitzhardinge Street
London W1H 0AH

ISBN 0-7134-7451-3

This book was designed and produced by
Quarto Publishing plc
6 Blundell Street
London N7 9BH

Senior Editor: Caroline Beattie
Editor: Susan Berry

Design: Richard Mellor
Picture Research: Ian Laurenson/Sarah Shreeves

Art Director: Moira Clinch
Art Editor: Philip Gilderdale
Publishing Director: Janet Slingsby
Picture Manager: Sarah Risley

With thanks to Mellor Design Ltd and Neal Cobourne

Typeset by Bookworm Typesetting, Manchester
Manufactured in Hong Kong by
Excel Graphic Arts Limited
Printed in Hong Kong by
Leefung-Asco Printers Limited

CONTENTS

INTRODUCTION

The purpose of any poster is primarily to attract attention, to be read at a distance and to convey the message in an appropriate idiom. For this poster, the designer has made use of brilliant primary colors, plus orange, contrasted with black, to create a vivid, modern and youthful poster for a music venue.

Four-color design is not the only option for creating a strong impact. A single color, cleverly used, can help to both gain and hold attention without being a strident element of the design. In this French poster, even small flashes of red bring an otherwise sober graphic poster to life, catching the eye and drawing it into the content.

In graphic design, color serves four principal functions:

- It attracts attention
- It holds attention
- It conveys information
- It makes information memorable

Attracting attention

For any design to do its job, it must first catch the attention. Color can be particularly successful in achieving this, for the following reasons.

As a rule, the designer has a relatively short space of time to capture the viewer's interest. Though human eyes can scan a wide area, the part of the field of vision which is *in focus* at any given moment is surprisingly small – roughly the area of a large coin held at arm's length. The normal experience of seeing everything in focus at all times is an illusion created by the mobility of the eye, which rotates to a new position on average some four or five times a second. Though color can be sensed more or less directly throughout the field of vision, only a restricted area at the centre of the gaze can read a word or formal symbol clearly.

As a result, when a large-scale display is examined, it is usually the color that first catches the eye, followed by a picture, then any formal symbol, trademark, logo, word or phrase. Color, in isolation or in combination, can be read immediately and from a greater distance than a shape, word, or pattern.

In packaging, book publishing, and poster and magazine design, color is often the single most eye-catching feature of the display. On average, a colored image can be expected to stimulate some 40 percent more interest than a comparable black and white or monochromatic version. When thumbing through a newspaper or periodical, we are almost invariably encouraged to stop and look by the inclusion of color.

On a well-stocked shelf, a great many colors and package designs compete for the shopper's attention, so color is especially helpful in picking out a familiar product from a group of similar goods, particularly since the standardization of modern retailing has reduced the variety of package sizes, shapes, and proportions.

On average, if we cannot find what we are looking for in five to six seconds, we will probably go after another product. Where the designer's first priority is to capture the viewer's attention, it may at first seem logical to assume that color combinations with the greatest degree of contrast and vividness are the most visible. This is not necessarily so. Colorful combinations of highly contrasting colors, such as yellow and violet, red and blue, and green and purple, may cancel each other out optically and may irritate and repel rather than attract. As a rule, strong differences of lighter against darker colors in a hard-edged design offer more compelling visual features and legible typography, as can be seen in road and traffic signs.

In daytime, color vision is normally most sensitive to yellow light, which is why yellow appears as the lightest and brightest color in the rainbow. Greatest visibility is offered by a combination of yellow and black, and it may be no accident that stinging insects have adopted this combination to startle predators. Other easily legible combinations, in order of greater to lesser impact, are white letters on a blue background, white on green, black on orange, black on yellow, black on white, white on red, red on yellow, green on white, and dark red lettering on a pale green ground.

Luminous or Dayglo paints offer greater visibility than normal surface colors and are therefore particularly useful in dangerous situations, or for life-saving instructions. The pigments of such paints (commonly zinc or calcium compounds) have the ability to absorb invisible ultraviolet energy from the sun and to release it slowly as visible light – hence their ability to glow in the dark. Phosphorescent orange life preservers and life jackets are particularly visible at dawn and dusk (when visibility is at its worst), since they then offer the greatest contrast to the deep blue sea.

For many commercial and non-commercial uses, such as hotel signs and traffic signals, (and, of course, in the dark) colored lights are more effective than colored surfaces in attracting the viewer's attention. Lights also give us a range of information. The red light on the left (port side) of a ship or plane in combination with a green light on the right (starboard) side tells us not only the location of the craft at night, but also its speed and direction of travel.

Holding attention

Having successfully, if briefly, halted the viewer's scanning eye, the designer's secondary intention is to hold his or her interest long enough to allow all relevant information to be read. The mere presence of color generates visual interest: colored words and images are consistently rated more attractive and individual than similar ones in black and white.

It has been estimated that for a package design on the supermarket shelf to halt a customer's attention it must do its job within one twenty-fifth of a second. A black-and-white advertisement must accomplish a similar task in less than two-thirds of a second, while a magazine advertisement which includes color normally holds the attention for an average of two seconds. With such restricted time spans, simplicity of color and composition in any design must be the rule.

Surveys indicate that a colored advertisement stimulates considerably greater interest than an uncolored one, although size, boldness of type, and location on the design are obviously important additional factors. In direct mailing, the inclusion of color in the mail-shot literature can draw up to 50 percent more replies than uncolored versions, although the "feel" of the paper and the quality of the printing have an influence in the response.

Whenever color is included in a design, it almost always becomes the focus of attention. A close examination of the eye reveals that its light-sensitive interior (the retina) possesses a tiny, central cavity, called the fovea. This is packed with a dense concentration of visual cells and is responsible for our ability to see fine detail in daylight.

In order to satisfy the need to see the world in focus at all times, the fovea has to be directed constantly to whatever is of immediate visual interest. Having momentarily bestowed its attention, the important question arises: how does the eye know where to look next?

A partial answer is that, several times each second, new information is collected from the "corner" of the eye – in reality a ring of less densely packed cells surrounding the fovea. Although this peripheral area of the inner eye is unable to see in focus, it is highly sensitive to movement, flicker, and dazzle.

When seen from a distance, a design must be eye-catching, inviting, clear, and easy to read. Ideally, the design should also encourage easy scanning so that the eye is led smoothly from one part of the design to another. Where a design is very regular, there is a danger that it may lose the viewer's interest too quickly. Whereas, if a design is too irregular, it may appear confusing or annoying and so interest is lost before the design has communicated its complete message.

When planning a graphic design or color composition of any kind, the designer would do well to consider carefully which color combinations are most suitable, and therefore most efficient, in arousing and sustaining the customer's curiosity. While the eye may be drawn to a package of breakfast cereal that demands attention with a combination of black or red lettering on a yellow ground, we would expect a perfume giftbox to be more gently persuasive. To encourage the customer to read and consider the contents of the design as a whole, the designer must consider where to direct the viewer's attention first, then second, then third, and so on. Such a well-ordered visual response is likely to avoid the confusion that would occur if several design elements were to compete simultaneously for the same amount of attention.

While the repetition of elements of equal importance is usually desirable in, say, a wallpaper or textile design, which has no "message," a balance of dominant against less-dominant features is needed in a graphic design to establish a hierarchy that promotes visual stability and visual clarity. In other words, there are stable points of focus from which the eye can explore the design in an orderly manner. Visual interest is then sustained by balancing the relative importance of combinations of color, shape, size, and texture within the design as a whole.

A major consideration in 20th-century design has been the relationship of the so-called "foreground" elements of a design with those of the "background." While normal visual perception involves emphasizing the foreground, usually at the expense of the background, designers must sooner or later develop an ability to hold and balance both simultaneously in the imagination.

In typography, for example, legibility depends on paying attention not just to letterforms but to the blank spaces in between and around them. This entails making careful choices of typeface,

In a very different context and style, red has been added as the single additional color, but by varying the tone and saturation a surprising colorful and lively design results, its impact increased by the asymmetric diagonal shapes and exciting typography.

Color can also be used to provide quick, easy-to-grasp visual codes. Here simple combinations of pattern and color have been used to identify particular branches of British Rail's various service groups as instantly recognizable logos (explained in detail in a manual for personnel).

Color can also be used to convey specific ideas or information, by association with the colors of well-known objects. In this poster for a French design exhibition in London, the red, white and blue of the French flag has been employed to evoke instantly an image of France, while for the range of air fresheners, the different fragrances "Alpine," "Exotique," and "Marine," for example, have been made readily identifiable by the greeny-blue mountain colors of the first, the hot reds and oranges of the second, and the deep sea blue of the third.

type size and color, and considering the overall texture of an area of text in order not to make it unduly difficult to read. In considering the legibility of printed type, contrasts of light against dark are generally more important than those of color identity or *hue* (see page 11) and colorfulness or *saturation* (see page 12). In other words, slogans and text are read more quickly and easily when there is a marked difference in *tone*, rather than hue and saturation, between the lettering and its background.

A strident color combination may be more inviting initially than a subdued one, but there is a danger that the viewer will tire of it more quickly. Where vividness of color is responsible for rapid visual fatigue (as would be the case in textbook typography) this can generally be considered a disadvantage. As a rule, a design exhibiting strong differences of tone will hold the viewer more readily than one in which tonal differences are slight. Strong contrasts of hue, such as red type on a green ground, may be readable from a distance if the letters are sufficiently large and bold. In small type and blocks of text, to be read from a normal reading distance of 13in (33cm), the same combination will probably exhibit a distracting or flickering effect. A popular solution when using small lettering is to set dark-colored type against a light, neutral or metallic background. In designing blocks of text, the most legible combination is black on white, followed by black on yellow, yellow on black, green on white, and red on white. Alternatively, the least legible color combinations include red on blue, orange on blue, yellow on orange, and green on orange, since their similarity of tone will usually give a dazzling impression.

When restricted to thin lines, colors can also change their identity. From a distance, yellow tends to appear white, orange to look red, green to look blue, and blue to appear black. If red type is set against a green or blue ground, an optical confusion occurs in which the colors cancel out each other's identity and appear gray or neutralized. The text itself is thrown out of focus, as also occurs when yellow type is printed on a white background or blue type is printed on a black ground.

A further critical factor is the influence of the intensity and color of the illuminating light. In daylight, human color vision is normally most sensitive to yellow light. When the eye is adapted to much lower levels of illumination – in other words when our eyes have got used to the dark – the greatest sensitivity shifts to green, and the eye becomes entirely blind to red light. As a result, a signboard displaying, for example, red lettering on a black background is acceptably legible in sunlight but appears uniformly black by moonlight. A preferable combination, such as pale green letters on a dark red background, would remain visible under both conditions.

Particular attention should therefore be given to designs (such as traffic signs) intended to be read by day and night, or under both high and low levels of artificial light. Other problems arise when the illumination is distinctly colored. A map or set of other instructions printed in red ink on white paper becomes entirely invisible under sodium yellow street lights or under the orange-red illumination of a photographic darkroom. In comparison to "white" daylight, the light from a tungsten filament bulb (used in normal table lamps) tends to make reds appear slightly brighter and blues duller. The same effect occurs under the warm white fluorescent tubes often used in supermarkets, while the opposite effect occurs under the harsher illumination of the cool white fluorescent lights often used in commercial situations.

Conveying information

It is also important to consider the direction of the light in relation to the viewer and object(s) being viewed.

In almost the same instant that a color catches and holds our attention, it must also succeed in communicating the relevant character and content of an object or image.

It is generally agreed that, of all the visual elements in art and design (shape, tone, texture, etc), color is the element which more directly affects our emotional records. Indeed, our subjective response to most visual imagery is based on the generally held belief that powerful correspondences exist between visual symbols and other aspects of human experience.

Many such experiences involve transfers between one of our senses and another – an effect known as synesthesia. In particular, visual images can evoke a wide variety of non-visual associations, such as those of taste, sound, and smell, and feelings of like or dislike, tension or relaxation. Testing the responses of large groups of people has established, for example, that a red-painted room is generally perceived as feeling warmer than a blue-painted one of the same temperature, that time seems to pass more quickly in a red room than a blue one, that sound generally seems louder in a white-walled room than a dark-walled one, and that memory functions best when a room is well-lit.

Common experience confirms that color can affect our subjective assessment of size, shape, weight, and distance. There is a tendency, for example, for a blue object to appear smaller and farther away than a red one of the same size and at the same distance. Similarly, a black package will tend to appear smaller, thinner, and heavier than an otherwise identical white package. In product design, where size and weight may be associated with value for money, such subliminal responses are important, since they can influence a decision to buy or not.

While such optical illusions can be responsible for misjudgments of color and size, it seems less believable that color is influenced by an object's meaning. However, a leaf shape cut from gray card may appear greener than a round disk cut from the same card. In one well-known survey, when groups of children were asked to estimate the size of small gray disks and silver coins, they accurately assessed the size of the disks, but all over-estimated the size of the coins.

Although no one can ever guarantee that a particular image will produce precisely the intended response, general agreements do exist, even when logic may dictate otherwise. Red, for example, has traditionlly been associated with fire, even though flames are generally not red and heat itself is invisible.

It can be to the advantage or disadvantage of author and publisher that a book is judged by its cover. In the retail store, we are often encouraged to judge the quality of a product by its package. Color, shape, and texture are known to be critical factors in the promotion of cosmetics, for example, and it may take an enormous investment of time, money, and market research to establish the right color combination, the right image, and the right face and figure for a new, exclusive perfume. Knowledge of the various choices and images promoted by competitors is another significant factor.

Color choice is a particularly important consideration in anticipating the taste and quality of food and drink. Freshness, nutrition, aroma, consistency, and texture are important, too, but where products are ready-packed they must often be assessed by visual clues alone. It is not uncommon to exploit color to enhance a product's appeal, a brown glass bottle, for example, being used to exaggerate the strength of a beer. As a rule, dark-colored labels or packages suggest strongly flavored foods (generally favored by adults) and light-colored labels imply greater subtlety of flavor. Label designs for low-alcohol or "lite" beers and wines, and diet soft drinks often utilize the paler tints of an established color combination to indicate their relationship to the associated, stronger or sweeter products.

When supermarkets began to produce their own generic brands, undecorated and uncolored packaging often succeeded in promoting the feeling of honesty and value for money. Nowadays, the practice is diminishing, although white, often combined with blue or black (otherwise unappetizing color choices), is still used for less expensive and bulky foods, such as refined sugar and flour, and to suggest hygiene in the packaging of milk, cheese, and margarine. Customers who can afford only a few purchases will enjoy the feeling that what they have been able to afford is substantial.

Making information memorable

Once a color combination has caught and held the attention, and helped to convey a suitable message, its final task in the retail store is to attach itself to a product. Ideally, it must encourage the customer to recognize and buy the product a second and third time. Often, when a package has done its job in the store, it may also need to continue to appear attractive on the kitchen or bathroom shelf, or in the playroom, office, or yard.

It is a matter of fact that color attracts attention, and a matter of degree that some color combinations hold the attention more than others. It is often a matter of speculation that one color combination will convey its message better than another, and a matter of chance that one set of colors will attach itself more or less permanently to one product rather than another.

There are many ways of making information memorable and color is one of the tools at the designer's disposal. Here the classic connotations of being "in the black" and "in the red" have been used to striking advantage for a bank's promotional literature. Logos are another simple way of putting over easily memorable information. Here, the bold primary colors and simple shapes of the logo for G.P. Decors fixes easily in the mind's eye, while displaying good "stand out" ability when read from a distance.

An equally arresting image has been used for an American University sorority society's literature, and the strong sweeping graphic image of the man and woman have been contrasted with repeating, simple, muted colored shapes in the background. Its subtle, low-key approach is in interesting contrast to these vibrant, but highly effective, label designs for a range of children's meals, where the designer has rightly opted for brilliant colors and striking, quite complex images, to appeal to children's known preferences for bright colors and "story"-style pictorial imagery.

In other words, though a particular color combination succeeds in visibility, legibility, and appeal, there is no guarantee that it will retain its association with a product or brand name. No hard-and-fast rules exist that allow us to link colors to particular judgmental or emotional states. Designers using color to attempt to influence the viewer's response are almost always working more in the realm of intuition than intellect, which is why creative design is more an art than a science. Even so, ignoring the results of methodical market research and refusing to comprehend the simpler principles of color theory would be a miscalculation.

In retailing, as on the sportsfield, color heightens emotional involvement, and the simple inclusion of color will help us remember what we have seen. Surveys of responses to advertizing consistently find that color promotes positive feelings toward advertized products, stimulates appetite for food and drink, and encourages greater decisiveness in choosing vacations to new destinations. It has been assessed that a colored advertisement has three to four times the retentive power of an uncolored one. Even so, while color is a major consideration, it must be supported by the right shape, size, texture, and content of an image or text.

The most memorable colors are those that are most easy to name. Although several thousand variations of color can be distinguished, the vocabulary to describe them is poor. It consists of relatively few color names: principally brown, red, orange, yellow, green, blue, violet, and purple, plus light, dark, and dull variations of each. These are augmented by neutral colors — white, gray, and black — and by a few easily identifiable metallic colors, notably gold, silver, bronze, and copper.

Simple, easily remembered color combinations are those most likely to be successful at encouraging repeated sales of certain brands. A bold color combination (such as deep blue and silver) is memorable while a subtle one (such as peach and lavender) may easily be forgotten. The retentive power of a color combination is most effective when the number of colors is limited. There should be little difficulty, for example, in remembering a red, green, and gold emblem or logo, though the "mood" of a more complex color combination may also make a memorable impression.

Two companies that have been particularly successful in sustaining their color identity are Eastman Kodak and Coca-Cola. Both were established in the 1880s, yet "Kodak yellow" and "Coca-Cola red" remain distinctive and immediately identifiable in a wide variety of contexts. When Kodak substituted blue for the yellow in 1914, its sales dropped significantly until the familiar yellow pack was reinstated. The shelf life of an advertizing campaign is usually about two months, while that of a package design can last as long as five years before some degree of restyling is necessary.

Memorized color combinations are particularly beneficial in promoting safety, and increasing the speed with which maps and certain types of other information can be read, absorbed, and recognized. Locating and understanding fire safety equipment, for example, is an important situation in which color codes can be used to attract attention and convey information as quickly and clearly as possible. Eye-catching red has traditionally been used for fire extinguishers. In the European standard, these contain water, while yellow cylinders contain foam for smothering flammable liquids and solids, black cylinders contain gas to control flammable liquids and gases, and blue extinguishers contain powder, suitable for all other hazards, including, for example, electrical fires.

Color forecasting takes account of previous and current preferences, market research, popular and less popular purchases, usage and attitude reports, and other opinions expressed by professionals in the field. Such rapidly shifting color trends often mirror the mood of the moment and prevailing social concerns, such as health and the environment. Though suspicious, the buying public has a constant appetite for the new and unfamiliar, so that novel color combinations have a good chance of catching the consumer's eye.

Color associations

Each of us has access to both personal and collective color associations. Personal color symbolism, influenced by age, gender, mood, and personal experience, can often be deduced by taking note of our regular choices of nonfunctional colors, such as those of favorite and frequently worn clothes.

As far as age is concerned, it is common for both the very young and the very old to enjoy vivid colors, rather than the muted tints which are often chosen for them. The generation that grew up in the 1960s and 1970s retains a general preference for vivid color. In the 1980s the most popular color among teenagers was black (symbolizing protest and diassatisfaction) and bleached blue (symbolic of boyishness or "tomboy" immaturity), occasionally augmented with brightly colored or fluorescent highlights.

Collective color associations are more likely to be influenced by cultural conventions and established traditions. Preferences can be expected to differ between one nationality and another. It is not unusual, for example, for the colors of a nation's flag to symbolize the allegiances and aspirations of its predominant cultural group. The presence of red in a flag might suggest revolution, socialism, or a predominantly Christian (especially Catholic) society. Yellow might represent intellect or wisdom, sun and sand, or optimism for the future. Green might emphasize nature and agriculture, or a predominantly Muslim society. Blue might represent spirituality, morality, or Puritanism, or simply sea or sky. White may represent peace, purity, or virtue, or neutrality between forces that were formerly in opposition.

Colors and their combinations thereby induce associative meanings that may have little to do with direct visual experience. Pinpointing selections of colors which evoke particular responses in the thoughts and feelings of the designer, client company, customer, and viewer is an important element of design. Shape, size, pattern, and texture are also important contributors to the overall effect, coupled with the intuitions of the designer and an awareness of past, present, and predicted trends.

Though the emphasis in advertizing is almost always on the positive nature of the product, it pays to remember that each family of colors has negative or positive associations. Red, for example, can represent vitality and excitement, courage, and enterprise, but it can also symbolize aggression, cruelty, agitation, and immorality. Equally, yellow can evoke sunshine, cheerfulness, radiance, and optimism, but the reverse of the same coin represents jealousy, cowardice, and deceit. Green symbolizes peace, balance, harmony, honesty, and prosperity, fertility, re-

generation, and growth; deeper green evokes tradition, reliability, and reassurance. The negative side of green has connotations of greed, envy, nausea, poison, and corrosion. Blue, on its positive side, is connected with efficiency, contemplation, order, and loyalty; on its negative side with feelings of depression and detachment, coldness and apathy.

In any design, therefore, the final choice of colors rests on several considerations. It is possible to select colors on a purely aesthetic basis, though ideally an agreeable and positive response is needed in the mind of the customer. Any hard-headed marketing person will insist on using the color most likely to sell the product to the targeted consumers.

To fulfill such a brief, the nature of the product, service, or event being promoted needs to be carefully analyzed, and may involve researching which combinations of color and form have proved successful in selling similar commodities elsewhere. A number of searching questions about the product have to be answered. Who is it aimed at – male, female, young, old, single or married? What national and social group does the consumer belong to? At what season is the product being marketed?, and so on.

Prior to choosing a suitable color or color combination, the designer must establish and clarify the quality and quantity of the information conveyed. A useful starting point is to invent a working title, using the section headings in this book, to help foster and fix a suitable image for the product or project.

Hue, tone, and saturation

In comparing two colors, one beside another, the difference in appearance that usually impresses you most is that between the redness, yellowness, greenness, or blueness of two colors. This difference is described as a difference in *hue*.

Nature boldly displays its full sequence of hues in the rainbow, with the exception of purple (a non-spectral color obtained by mixing together the red and violet extremes of the spectral color sequence). When all possible hues are arranged around the edge of a circle, purple can be positioned conveniently between the red and violet to create a continuous sequence of hues, known usually as a *color wheel*.

Do's and Don'ts for designing packs worldwide

France, Holland & Sweden:
Green is associated with cosmetics.

Europe generally:
Designs resembling the swastika are generally disliked.

France:
Red is masculine. To the rest of the world, blue is masculine. Avoid illustrations showing liquor being poured.

Holland:
Avoid using German national colors.

Ireland:
Green and orange should be used with care.

Sweden:
Swedes do not like packaging showing gold or blue. Combinations of white and blue, the colors of the National flag, are best avoided. Consumers do not like giant packs. The brand name must be pronounceable in Swedish.

Switzerland:
Yellow means cosmetics. Blue means textiles. The oval is an omen of death.

Turkey:
A green triangle signifies a free sample.

Arab countries:
Take care when using green because it has Moslem connotations. Avoid designs incorporating a cross.

Buddhist countries:
Saffron yellow indicates priests.

The East generally:
Yellow means plenty. Yellow and pink together connote pornography.

Eastern Asia:
Avoid the circle as it has connotations of the Japanese flag.

Ivory Coast:
Dark red indicates death.

Latin America:
Purple indicates death.

Moslem countries:
Green is a holy color and should be used with care. (Most Moslem countries have green in their flags.)

Source: Richard Head, Siebert/Head Ltd.

This shows how the principal hues relate to each other. Colors opposite each other (such as red and green) on the color wheel are referred to as complementary colors. Blue, red and yellow are the primary colors.

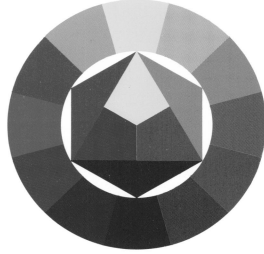

Tone and saturation

This box, which shows the permutations in tone (top row = lightest, bottom row = darkest) and in saturation. The color is fully saturated when it is unmixed with white or black. The fully saturated hues of these colors can be spotted, as they are the brightest in each vertical row.

The so-called primary colors are fundamental hues which can be used to obtain, by mixture, a wide variety of other colors, but which cannot themselves be obtained by this process. When mixing together beams of colored light, the three ideal primary colors are red, green, and blue. When mixing together amounts of colored paints, inks, or dyes, especially those used by the printer and color photographer, the three ideal primary colors, also known as the process colors, are purple (commonly called *magenta*), yellow, and turquoise-blue (commonly called *cyan*).

In comparing two colors, one beside another, one color may appear lighter or darker than the other. This can be identified as a difference of *tone* or *value*. For surfaces that have been painted or printed, this can extend from the palest of tints to the darkest of shades of the same hue. A painter can easily change the tone of a color by adding white to make it lighter or black to make it darker. The printer has either to add transparent extender to the colored ink to make it lighter, or reduce the percentage (or dot size) of the half-tone screen.

While hue is useful for discerning important differences between the aesthetic or appealing qualities of one object against another (the difference between a red or green tomato, for example) differences in tone, such as the highlight or shadow in a black-and-white photograph, for example, are valuable for providing information about form, shape, weight, texture, and volume.

In comparing two colors, one beside another, one color may appear more or less vivid than another. This can be identified by the terms *saturation* or *colorfulness*. Saturation, also known as chroma or chromatic intensity, can extend from the exceptional purity of the colors of the rainbow to the colorlessness of a neutral surface that appears white, black, or gray. The painter can easily change the degree of saturation by mixing a vivid hue (straight from the tube) with varying amounts of gray paint. The printer, using transparent inks in combination with half-tone screens, needs greater ingenuity in carefully matching the percentages of the process colors to achieve the same result.

In general, our memory of hue is poor and largely symbolic. A symbol often consists of a standardized idea used to unite a large number of variations on a theme. Hence the word "red" can conjure in our imagination the color located on the outer arc of the rainbow, a "stop" traffic signal, or the color of a ripe strawberry, without needing to be too specific about its exact tint, or shade, or degree of saturation. For the most part, the remembered symbol is enough.

In casual descriptions of colors it is often enough to describe the grass as "green," the sky as "blue," and the rooftops as "red." A closer look might reveal that long grass is more brown than green, or that (even on the sunniest of summer days) the sky is not always very blue, and that the red of the lit side of the rooftop is distinctly different from the red on its shadowed side. In other words, there is a strong tendency to remember colors as being more saturated than they actually are. Importantly, for designers whose work is intended to appeal to the general public, these exaggerated and/or simplified associations are the ones that need to govern our images whenever drawings or photographs of familiar objects are used on the printed page or package. Generally speaking, we tend to believe that the colors of an object – such as a leaf or a mailbox – "actually" remains the same whether it is seen in sunlight, in shadow, or at night by streetlight.

Though it is often an advantage that our memory of the actual coloring of objects is poor, symbolic, or exaggerated, there are at least two sets of situations in which we promptly become aware if the color varies only slightly from the norm: the complexion of the skin, and the coloring of food.

Manufacturers and advertizers soon learn that food packaged and offered for sale must conform in terms of colors to the customer's expectations. In this respect, enhanced color is sometimes used to suggest greater freshness, sweetness, energy, or potency. Dark and dull colors are more suggestive of cooked and savory foods than lighter-colored foods, and dark-colored beers (such as Guinness) give the impression of having stronger alcohol content than lighter-colored beers. In other contexts, dull or faded colors may give the negative impression that the goods have been on the shelf too long.

When a photograph of any typical object or natural feature needs retouching, it is important to remember that it is often to the heightened saturation of a memorized image that the picture must appeal, rather than its actual coloring.

It is important to acknowledge that all color comparisons are *relative*, and that the brain often compensates for inconsistencies. For example, the striking change in color that occurs when a photograph or object is carried from a dark interior into broad daylight usually goes unnoticed, since the overall *relationship* between its colors and tones remains more or less the same in both situations.

About This Book

Graphic designers using color in their work not only have to understand the principles previously described in this introduction, they also have to use color in conjunction with other graphic forms, including the chosen imagery and typography. Creating a harmonious balance between the various elements in the design – form or structure, illustration style, photography or artwork and typography and, of course, color – is what the designer's work is all about, and an understanding of each element, and how it interacts with the others, is a major part of graphic design training.

This book has broken down the various ways color is used in graphic design into six basic elements, which to some extent overlap with the concepts mentioned above. They are: color associations; combinations of hue, tone, and saturation; shapes and edges; size and proportion; and pattern and texture. These concepts have then been discussed in a range of applications that are often used to sum up the perceived market or "angle" of a particular design – popular, exclusive, individual, corporate and so on, so that designers can see at a glance how various combinations of color or patterns can be used to create, enhance or emphasize the message they are trying to convey.

By arranging contrasting concepts on the same spread – romantic versus classical, modern versus traditional – the designer can see more clearly the distinction between them, and how color has been used to reinforce these concepts.

Although some of the interpretations are bound to be subjective, others are more closely rooted in fact. Blue would be universally perceived as a colder color than orange, for example. To some extent different effects can be achieved by combining or contrasting elements that oppose each other, or even cancel each other out, thereby creating a more subtle or more complex message.

Obviously, in order to make the associations of color work well in graphic design, designers have to start with a clear idea of the message that they are trying to get across. Any design, no matter how well executed, will founder if the designer has not fully grasped the purpose at the initial briefing, and no amount of sophisticated understanding of the messages that can be conveyed by manipulating color will work unless this basic principle is clearly understood.

Graphic design is, after all, a means of communicating ideas. The more clearly the designer understands both the purpose of the design, and the sometimes hidden psychological messages, as conveyed by color, amongst other factors, the more likely the design is to hit its target.

USING EACH CHAPTER

Color Associations

Observation and expectation play a large part in the ways in which we associate colors with particular objects – to the point where the color itself takes on the characteristics of that object. Because fire is red and water is blue, we tend to perceive red as a warm color and blue as a cool one. Traditionally, yellow is associated with sunshine and is therefore used extensively on the packaging of cereal products. Green is now the color of environmental awareness. Less obvious associations are caused by a range of different objects and experiences, and designers need to take this into account when planning color in their work.

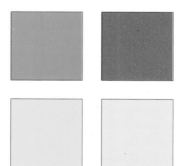

Although red is universally considered to be a warm color and blue a cool one, yellow (which falls between them in the color wheel – see page 12) can be perceived as either, depending on the degree of red (left) or blue (right) that it contains. Darker or lighter tones and fuller or lesser saturations can change our perceptions about a color. A highly saturated mid-blue can appear very active, while a darker blue, of the same hue, can appear passive.

Combinations of Hue

Very few designs are restricted to one color. As soon as more than one color is used, designers need to think carefully about the effect of their chosen combinations, not only in terms of the atmosphere or mood the choice creates, but in terms of legibility where typography is included in the overall design. Using natural imagery to sell, say, wholewheat flour, a range of earth colors – golds, greens, oranges and browns – may be employed to conjure up the image of harvest, for example. Yet not all the colors will combine well to allow any typography to read properly.

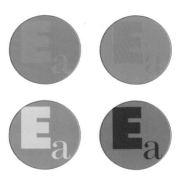

In each chapter we have used a bold sanserif capital letter together with a fine serif lower case typestyle to demonstrate the way that readability is affected by the use of different color combinations. Fine lines printed from the four process colors can suffer from register problems which are of course visually disturbing, so care must be taken to select appropriate typefaces and colors. Neutral black or white may be one alternative to achieve legibility without significantly altering the mood of the design.

Tone and Saturation

Color is affected by the degree of purity (saturation or brightness) and by its reflectivity (lightness or darkness of tone), changing not only the effect a particular hue may have on the beholder, but also affecting the legibility.

A mid-saturated, mid-toned blue might appear fairly passive, but as soon as the saturation is increased it takes on a much more active feel. Similarly, a light-toned green might have a feminine feel, but a darker-toned version of the same hue might well be more appropriate for a corporate image.

Dark tone   Mid tone   Light tone

Full saturation   Mid saturation   Low saturation

The particular hues of blue and red used here in their normal mid-toned, mid-saturated form would be impossible to read clearly. But, as can be seen, as soon as the tone of one is lightened, or the saturation altered, legibility improves.

Many designers often think and work solely in black and white, translating their designs into color only prior to going to press. This can result in some expensive mistakes, especially where legibility is a primary concern. Simply by altering either the tone or the saturation of a color, readability can be achieved without sacrificing the mood created by the original color combination.

Shapes and Edges

The way that colors are contained can alter the impression they make. A clear, cold, unpatterned plain blue contained in a square presents a more clinical and masculine impression than the same blue contained in a warmer circle or ellipse form. Different shapes and edges therefore affect the way that we perceive different colors, and can be manipulated to reinforce a particular message or to contradict it. Equally, organic or handmade forms have a strongly naturalistic feel, for example, while geometric, hard-edged shapes seem more artificial.

The shapes created by the letter forms in typography are an important factor in the atmosphere of the design. Compare, for example, the two shown here, the bold, sans serif letter being clearly masculine and the ornate italic character definitely feminine.

The above shapes for warm and cool are the more obvious shapes associated with flickering flames and water droplets but these sorts of simple devices, together with appropriate color schemes help designers create the right feel when communicating an idea.

Size and Proportion

Although the degree of saturation plays a part in the brilliance of any color, within a design the proportion of the colors used, and their relationship to each other is equally important. We perceive colors differently, depending on which colors are adjacent. For example a square of yellow on a white ground appears larger than a square of yellow on a black ground.

The proportions in which colors are used within a design affects not only our perception of the colors themselves but the atmosphere. Dark colors at the base of the design create a feeling of weightiness, and stability. Light colors at the base of a design, with darker colors above, produce a curiously top-heavy impression. Even proportions of colors tend to have a passive effect, while strongly contrasting colors produce a more active impression. Juxtaposing different colors also changes the impression of brightness, and allows some colors to recede and others to advance. For example, a small typesize in a contrasting color to its background can have as much impact as large letters on a tonally similar color background.

Pattern and Texture

Broken fragments of different colors present a very different image from a surface with a uniform color, and the forms of the pattern and nature of the texture can be used to alter or enforce particular color association messages. Equally the reflectivity or mattness of the texture enhances or reduces the impact of the color, changing the way it is perceived.

Different styles of pattern tend to evoke particular eras or moods. More particularly some patterns are definitely unsuitable for evoking a specific mood or atmosphere. A tiny flower pattern design is highly unlikely to be used on a product sold directly to men, but would be very suitable for a product aimed at the feminine market. The perception of a pattern or a texture can change dramatically with the colors used around it and thus it is best to experiment with a range of patterns and textures to achieve the right effect.

These traditional and modern images of a naturalistic leaf pattern and an abstract, geometric shape show how, even using the same color, you can affect the way it is perceived by the pattern imposed on it.

COOL

Coolness tends to imply distance, detachment, and aloofness in graphic design, and the "cool" sectors of the color wheel – the blues and greens, together with monochrome white, gray, and black – are often used to evoke suitable images of cold water, icy landscapes, and wintry scenes to sell products associated with cleanliness and hygiene, for example.

The impact of a clean-edged abstract design would be strengthened by using cool colors and softened by using warm ones, and designers can play on these contradictions between form and color to create interesting tensions in their work.

Shiny metallic surfaces and smooth, glossy papers generally give a much cooler impression than matte or textured ones, as do modern sanserif typefaces.

chilled
serene
wintry
restrained
reserved
refreshing
luminescent
mercurial
distant

heated

energetic

summery

affectionate

enthusiastic

appetizing

incandescent

jovial

welcoming

The colors associated with heat, warmth, and sunshine are the yellows, oranges, golds, and reds. Unlike the passive cool tones of blue and green, these tend to come forward off the page and play an active and demanding role – in the case of bright reds, sometimes even an aggressive one.

Texture is also strongly associated with warmth; the more patterned and rougher a surface is, the warmer its appearance. Thick, tinted papers are often used to give an impression of warmth, as is sepia ink. These reduce the otherwise sharp contrasts of black ink and white paper.

Natural, curling and twining shapes also give a warmer impression than squared-off or geometric forms, particularly when combined with figurative as opposed to abstract patterns.

WARM

Color Associations

The cool colors – blue and green – evoke the pale, bleached winter sky, distant shadows, or the reflections from the surface of water, snow, or ice. While warm colors imply cozy fireside comfort, cool colors suggest exposure to the elements – sea, sky, and landscape. Although coolness may at first seem less appealing, it can be put to good use to promote products with positive cool associations, such as winter wear, ski clothes, or varieties of frozen food. Deeper blues and greens are often used to promote concepts related to cleanliness and hygiene.

Cool colors are also typically used for promoting the freshness of dairy products or thirst-quenching drinks, for example, as well as pharmaceuticals and cosmetics, and electrical gadgets for the bathroom or kitchen.

Left: Every element of this poster design contributes to a sense of cool sophistication appropriate to the subject – a gliding contest. The blue-violet color range and image of a sleek plane wing make direct and indirect associations with the ideas of sky, flying, coolness, and open space. The spaciousness is emphasized by the broad white surround and the arrangement of the typography, which is generously letterspaced.

Above: This mineral water label design could not be more explicit in its use of the cool blues and greens as an instantly recognizable association with water. The water-color technique increases the cool, watery effect, and even the typography has been executed in blues and greens.

COOL

Above: The deep, rich swirling chocolate brown background, coupled with the simple, clear-cut white typography sends the message that this is a quality dessert aimed at a discerning, but not exclusive, market.

The warm colors strongly suggest images of physical and emotional warmth. The golden colors reminiscent of sunshine and sandy beaches are useful in promoting swimwear, suntan lotions, summer clothes, or vacations in tropical climates. The orange range of colors can represent the physical warmth of the fireside in winter, while the pinks and golds are associated with the soft warmth of skin.

The different associations are particularly important when advertising and packaging food and drink. Colors found to be most stimulating to the appetite are warm reds, oranges, and browns, and variations of these colors are widely used to sell cereals, cookies, and TV dinners, hot drinks, and alcohol such as brandy, and other after-dinner drinks. Elsewhere warm hues are, unsurprisingly, good for selling heat appliances, such as irons, hairdriers, microwave ovens, and fan heaters, and for products connected with warmth of touch, like cuddly toys, carpets, and soft furnishings.

Left: Browns and reds are appetizing colors directly associated with the idea of hot drinks. The red-brown of this tea packet is from the warmest range of brown hues and is used unambiguously throughout the pack, with no hint of a cool or opposite color. Solid color areas are complemented by gentle vignetted tones in the image on the front of the pack that also suggests softness, comfort and warmth.

Combinations of Hue

It is a common psychological response to describe certain hues as "cool" and others as "warm," although there is little basis in fact for this division. In general the cool hues extend from the blue-greens of sea green and verdigris at one extreme through the mid-blues to indigo and deep blue-violet at the other. The coolest of the colors in the color wheel is a greenish blue known by many names including aquamarine, turquoise blue, or kingfisher blue, typified at full-strength by the printer's process blue, cyan.

Most colors can be cooled by adding a touch of blue to them, so the yellows with a hint of blue turn a cooler limy green, and the reds with added blue have a purplish tinge like the printer's process red, magenta.

Rainbeau.

Right: Blue and white suggest hygiene and health and this is a combination often used for the packaging of dairy products. The design of this carton adds a strong green, equal in saturation and coolness to the blue, introduces a suggestion of vegetable freshness. Again the green, white, and yellow combination proves successful — it evokes freshness — all important in food packaging. The strong mid-green hue acts as a good contrast to the white and yellow lettering. The design is clean and functional: the two colors stand out clearly on the white ground and are combined effectively in both the image and the typography to promote the idea that the product is an essential part of a healthy diet.

Left: The use of cool green and white, with touches of blue and yellow for this natural yoghurt pack emphasizes the naturalness of the product, while the simple, clear white type of the branding echoes the purity of the contents.

Above: Perrier's cool green bottle and label combining crisp green, white, and yellow, are an important aspect of its immediately recognizable brand image. The colors are refreshing and suggest the purity of the product. In this poster, the greens are offset by a cool gray background reminiscent of a rainy sky, which relates directly to the copy line. This gray reflects through the neck of the green bottle, creating a visual link.

COLOR VARIATIONS

Blues, blue-greens, and lime-tinged yellows are among the coolest colors in the spectrum. Cool combinations imply: Cleanliness, thoughtfulness, aloofness.

Right: The images in this advertisement for leisure footgear suggest recreation and travel to exotic locations, emphasized by a hot, vivid color scheme in which all the main colors are selected from the warm part of the spectrum. Although the beige areas indicate shadow, they retain their warmth. The smaller motifs, such as the palm tree and moon symbols, introduce cool color accents that create points of contrast, so the intense, hot colors do not cancel each other out. The brand name is cleverly emphasized by the use of red isolated on a white panel.

The warm colors are principally centered on yellow-orange, orange, and orange-red, deepening into browns and ochers at one end and dull purples and violets at the other.

Though warmth is most powerfully suggested by hues in the orange-red sector of the wheel, all colors have their "warm" and "cool" extremes. The warm yellows extend from primary process yellow toward orange-reds, but exclude limy and lemony yellows. Although the blue-greens are cool, the warmer greens with a strong hint of yellow, and the warmer blues with a touch of red belong more to the warm than the cool sector.

Earth colors, yellow with a hint of red, and greens with a hint of yellow are all warm colors. Warm combinations imply: Friendliness, reassurance, edibility.

Right: An impression of evening light conveyed by the choice of muted colors from the warm range of the spectrum appropriately suggests that the club is a gathering spot for after-sundown relaxation. A warm blue is included in the design, applied to the flamingo motifs on each side – a cooler, lighter blue would create too high a contrast, drawing attention away from the central emphasis of the lettering and the silhouetted palm-leaf shapes.

Tone and Saturation

Blues and greens in their paler tones are commonly used for products associated with water and cleanliness: for the coloring of soaps and bath oils, shampoos, and shower gels, for example. Equally the cool, almost translucent tones of pale blues, light greens, and the cooler lemon yellows are used to evoke certain tangy or sharp flavors, such as those associated with lemon-lime, Pernod, or anisette, for example.

The deeper saturations or darker tones of the blues and greens are less cool-looking, so if you are trying to achieve, say, an association with winter, you should opt for bleached blues and greens, reminiscent of icy landscapes.

Fortunately for graphic designers, the paler cool colors are easy to achieve in any printing process. Fully saturated process cyan, however, should be used with care since it ceases to look particularly cool, and has a raw, aggressive look that is particularly well suited to bold punk graphics, for example. As the paler saturations and tones of blues and greens are passive and recessive, they can be valuable for creating cool backgrounds.

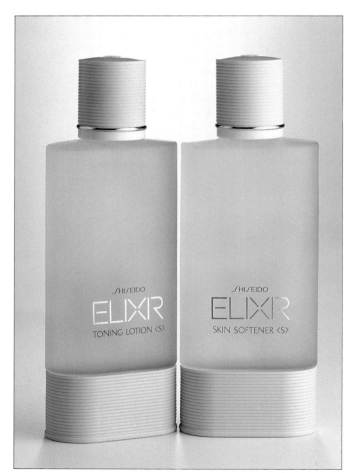

Above: Coolness is inherent in both the pale pastel green of this bottle and its teardrop shape. The extent of the light-toned green, with white bands on label and cap, dominates the stronger colors used in the image on the label – the dark blue lettering and the orange of the fruit. The label is clearly legible, but it is the cool, clean effect of the overall shape that is immediately striking.

Left: The use of very pale tones throughout the packaging of these cosmetic products creates a clean, sophisticated presence dependent on the bottle shape and subtly modified by effects of light and shade. In keeping with this restrained design, the typographic style is fine and elegant. The gold acts as a highlight when catching the light (on the blue bottle) or a dark shadow (on the green bottle), remaining legible in both cases.

COLOR VARIATIONS

Dark tone

Mid tone

Light tone

Full saturation

Mid saturation

Low saturation

Top: Pale tones tend to look cooler than dark tones, and give a feeling of space, lightness, and aloofness.

Above: Lower saturations of color tend to look cooler than the higher ones.

Left: Equatorial heat is effectively suggested by an unambiguously warm orange against black, set off by its contrasting complementary turquoise and reinforced by vivid red. The design is dominated by warm, rounded shapes and glowing color contrasts. The saturation of all colors is enhanced by the black background, and even converted to monochrome (above), the image remains strong and clearly readable.

An easy way to lend instant warmth to any color scheme is to view it through a pale orange or pink filter. The lighter toned and less saturated reds, bronzy oranges and soft pinks give the impression of warmth, with their associations with sunshine and summer.

In advertising it is important to understand that it is to such memorized preferences for highly saturated colors, rather than to the actual color of objects, that our advertising should usually appeal.

On a technical level, designers should bear in mind that it is hard to achieve a dilution of bright red in the four-color printing process, and a strong bright orange simply cannot be produced in four-color printing, although it presents no problems when using premixed inks.

COLOR VARIATIONS

Dark tone

Mid tone

Light tone

Full saturation

Mid saturation

Low saturation

Above: The warm brown of this wrapper suggests wholesomeness and gives the product a substantial feel. Its appeal is enhanced by the gradation of color from dark brown through orange to yellow, which creates tonal interest, although the colors are of similar saturation. Legibility is ensured by the white strip bearing the product name and white outlining of the nuts that provide the descriptive image.

Top: Pale tones of warm colors tend to look softer and more gentle, and are ideal for baby products.

Above: High saturations of warm colors are often used to indicate strength as well as warmth.

Shapes and Edges

The use of hard, clean edges in graphic designs can suggest scientific precision, and is a reassuring choice in, say, the promotion of over-the-counter medicines. Cool colors, such as the light-toned and desaturated blues, enhance these associations. Bottled mineral waters may use hard-edged blue labeling and blue caps and seals in combination with teardrop-shaped containers to suggest both purity and the thirst-quenching nature of the product.

Combinations of smooth and jagged, soft and hard, or opaque and translucent shapes in pale colors are reminiscent of snow-falls, melting ice, and winter skies, and can be used for products with "cool" connections.

Sanserif typography offers a cooler, more clinical approach than ornate curly faces, and contrasts of blue and white, and blue and black typography have a classic, understated appeal.

Right: This image has a literal association with snow-capped mountain peaks and jagged icicles, but the abstract elements are also designed to convey an immediate impression of coldness, height, and remoteness. Geometric shapes are typically cool and impersonal and the range of blues emphasizes a sense of distance.

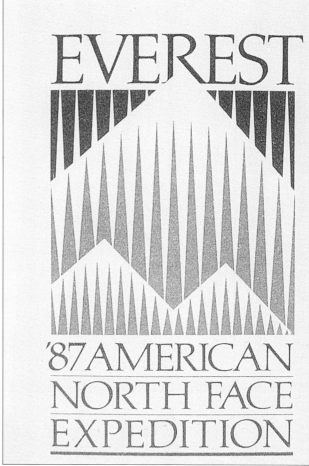

Above: The teardrop shape is the dominant cool shape, used here in effective combination with a cool color range. This is a small package that needs an eye-catching design, and the variation of colors is lively. The shapes are fluid but hard-edged, giving clarity to the color contrasts, and the design is cleverly managed so that the forms of an eye and eyebrow subtly emerge.

COLOR VARIATIONS

The forms – the shapes and edges – that confine different colors affect our perception of them. Coolness is usually suggested by:
- hard edges
- square, spiky shapes
- sanserif typefaces

Large, rounded objects and soft-edged forms imply the warmth associated with intimacy and femininity. Generous, circular and convex shapes are particularly suggestive of warmth, whereas thin, insubstantial concave forms create the opposite impression. Rounded shapes also tend to be reminiscent of food, suggesting luscious, exotic tropical fruit and warm baked breads and rolls, and may also evoke images of personal comfort – soft cushions and pillows, blankets and cuddly toys.

Rounded, soft-edged shapes also imply life and animation, while softly blended and soft-edged colors, created by air-brushing, blending pastels or watercolor washes, help to create a "warmer" atmosphere.

Above: Rounded shapes are warm and comforting, and the drawing style applied to these cuddly toys gives them a friendly aspect. There is a soft-edged quality to the line that implies gentle contours and furry texture, and the overall impression is conveyed by the bold, warm coloring. The type shows how the warm/cool contrast can be used to make type legible.

Right: The angle at which the dish and spoon are seen gives full emphasis to their roundness, so that the enveloping shapes and hot colors draw the viewer into a sense of comfort and nourishment. The curving letterforms of the Campbell's logo also evoke a warmth aptly associated with hot foods.

COLOR VARIATIONS

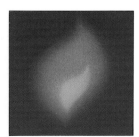

The forms – the shapes and edges – that confine different colors affect our perception of them. Warmth is often suggested by:
- soft-edged shapes
- serif and italic typefaces
- rounded shapes

Size and Proportion

Designs for books, packages, posters, and album covers, for example, usually conform to a predetermined set of measurements. Given such limitations, it is still possible, by manipulating the relative proportions of color and form of the component parts of the design, to suggest differing size and scale.

Wide or horizontal formats of pale greens and blues extending across a billboard, a printed page, or a double spread can project an expansive and significantly different image from the intimacy of limited areas of, say, deep blue restricted only to a small or vertical portion of the design. As a rule, pale or light blue areas will tend to appear larger while a similar-sized area of dark blue seems smaller and weightier.

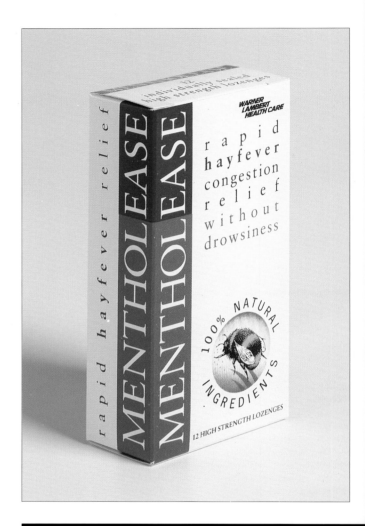

Right: A small pack needs uncluttered design. The color panel giving the product name draws immediate attention and running it lengthwise makes it possible to print the name fairly large. The colors relate to the words – green for the mint of menthol and a cool blue suggesting ease and a clear head. The proportions of the colors within the band are dictated by this division of the word, but this is balanced by featuring the blue more prominently in the type lines on the front of the pack.

Left: The proportions of the bottle are accentuated by the tonal gradation of its coloring, which adds height but makes it seem solidly grounded. Most of the design activity is at the centre of the shape. The lemon yellow dot helps to explain the contents of the bottle: its bright color stands out clearly against the green, so it need only form a small shape in the design and is used to dot the "i" in Sprite.

COLOR VARIATIONS

How a color is perceived is determined by the colors that surround it, and partly by the size and proportion of the colors relative to each other. Differing proportions have been used here to show some of the effects that can be achieved as a result.

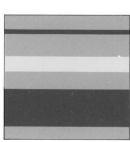

Above: Round shapes imply friendliness, just as rich reds and browns convey warmth. This simple cylindrical packaging for drinking chocolate uses both these elements to put across the concept of a warming, soothing, and relaxing drink. The typography style and the image of the cup and toaster have a flavor, signifying a reassuring tradition.

Right: The size of this label is, in practical terms, dictated by the shape of the bottle whose generous proportions it has been designed to emphasize. Dark tone at the bottom and light at the top give a feeling of weight. Rich, warm colors are used throughout except for the product name: bright hues give legibility to the type against the shaded red ground.

In nature, the deep, warm colors, such as red earths, brown ochers and leaf greens, appear as foreground colors, while the pale cool colors of sea or sky tend to extend away from us, eventually blending with the horizon. We rapidly become adept at using such information to make accurate judgements about distance, but rarely question the sophistication of the visual processes concerned.

Warmth may be suggested by apparently radiant, flamelike shapes, such as the price or special offer information often added to package designs, usually in vivid yellows or orange-reds, which tend to appear larger than they actually are. In general, saturated yellow and orange designs give the illusion of generosity and of expanding and advancing toward the viewer, while those that are predominantly blue or violet appear to recede and look smaller.

COLOR VARIATIONS

How a color is perceived is determined by the colors that surround it, and partly by the size and proportion of the colors relative to each other. Differing proportions have been used here to show some of the effects that can be achieved as a result.

WARM

27

Pattern and Texture

Although all the objects in a room are likely to be roughly the same temperature, some feel warmer or colder to the touch than others. This is because hard, metallic surfaces readily conduct the heat of the hand while softer fabric surfaces tend to conserve it. With this in mind the use of cold colors in labeling on packaging can be reinforced by a thoughtful selection of materials and textures.

Engraved metal or machine-made patterns, coupled with polished silver, steel, chrome, or mirrored surfaces, are also suggestive of coolness. In general, glossy surfaces feel cooler than matte ones. The appeal of a cool drink on a hot day could therefore be enhanced by the visual associations of a blue and silver label, a metallic seal, and a smooth glass bottle.

Spot varnishing may also be used on card to isolate areas of gloss on an otherwise matte-printed color image or surface.

Right: Fine gray and white vertical stripes create a cool, classical feeling well suited to a lager aimed at the upscale customer; touches of mid green and blue add to this coolness. There is an overall impression of silvered elegance because the package design leaves the metallic caps of the bottles openly displayed – real tactile qualities as well as visual effects are important elements of design.

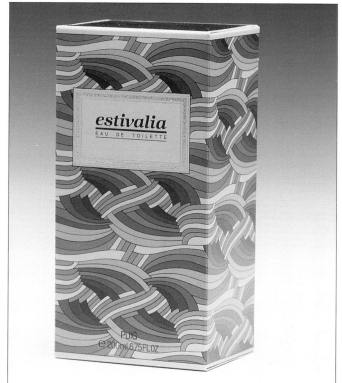

Right: A luxury item, designed to refresh and revitalize the user, is given a stylishly restrained yet colorful package with a fascinating wave-like pattern. The complex linear interaction of the pattern motif gains depth and clarity from the color range. All colors are chosen from the cool side of the spectrum, but they are varied in characteristics of hue and tone.

COLOR VARIATIONS

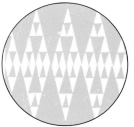

Cool patterns tend to be sharp, geometric, hard-edged, and repetitive – often in black and white – or without strong contrasts.

COOL

Representations of warmth produced by variations of color, shape, edge, and proportion can usually be enhanced by appropriate choices of pattern and texture, such as repetitions of flame shapes or radiating sunbursts, or by ribbed, ridged textures evocative of warmer knitted or woven textiles. Matte, non-glossy surfaces tend to look warmer, and wood is clearly warmer, both to the touch and visually, than shiny aluminum.

A wooden cigar box and an aluminum drinks container, for example, both give the impression of being appropriate for their contents.

Above: The rich good cooking of Victorian times is brought to life in these packages for Effie Marie's gourmet cakes. The overall wallpaper-like background, with echoes of the Arts and Crafts movement, in rich warm golds, reds and browns gives a hint of the smell of home-baking and is well-suited to the image of traditional good-quality food.

COLOR VARIATIONS

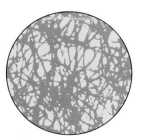

Warm patterns are often all-over irregular, fuzzy, and asymmetric designs, with rounded or soft shapes, and in toning colors.

Right: This Belgian chocolate dessert package uses all the colors in the warm section of the color wheel in an overall design that wraps around the carton. The stylized figures, reminiscent of 1950s comics, convey the impression of youthful zest for life, ideally suited to a product aimed mainly at children.

The cool colors of the spectrum – the blues and greens – are generally perceived as passive and indeed they tend to recede when viewed from a distance. The feeling of passivity that they induce can be exploited for its own sake to sell certain products or services – generally those that aim to reassure or convince, such as the health or savings programs of insurance companies and banks – or the more passive colors can be used to tone down an otherwise vigorous design to lend it stability. Dufy used the coolness of blues to great effect in his paintings, contrasted with strokes in sketched outlines.

Organized shapes and repeating patterns create a more passive feeling in a design, which can be enhanced by avoiding sharp tonal contrasts.

inert

static

restful

tranquil

relaxing

phlegmatic

calming

still

docile

alert

dynamic

restive

animated

stimulating

sanguine

invigorating

responsive

lively

There are many instances where a designer may seek to create an intensely lively, vibrant and vigorous image – for the covers of children's adventure stories, for pop music album covers, or for sports promotions. Fully saturated warm colors will help to emphasize this aspect of the design, and strong contrasts – (golds and purples), or even clashes (orange and pink) will help to give tne design life and movement.

Texture and pattern can be used effectively to enhance an impression of vitality – using short staccato strokes or whirling patterns – as can the use of strong tonal contrasts or saturations of color.

Random patterns and jigsaw shapes also help to break up the design and give it life and movement.

ACTIVE

Color Associations

Passivity suggests restfulness, calm, and reassurance. A typically passive combination of saturated greens, blues, and grays is ideal for promoting commodities with connotations of relaxation and rest, such as herbal medicines, skin lotions and creams, or bath oils, for example.

Passive color combinations make a good choice of background for jobs requiring calm and concentration or for promotional material aimed at putting across the image of contemplation, thoughtfulness, and organization. In general, combinations of grayed or muted colors are particularly good as a neutral background for brighter, more eye-catching colors, because the passive colors have a natural tendency to recede.

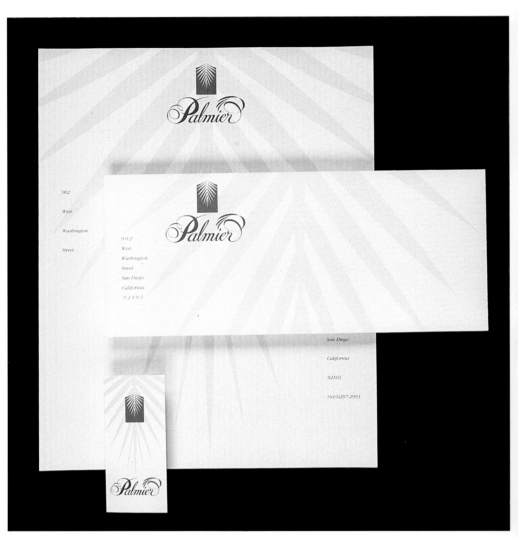

CIRCLE OF SUPPORT©

Left: Muted hues and darker tones tend to be more passive than brighter saturations. Adding black to any color renders it more passive, as can the choice of shapes – here the solid, stable triangle is contained and balanced within the softer, rounded form of the circle.

Above: Cool colors are generally thought to create a relaxed atmosphere. In this logo design and stationery for a Californian bistro, a simplified color palette – muted tones of green and gray – and a spare but elegant graphic symbol of a palm leaf have been used to create a distinctly sophisticated, modern, and cool image. The feeling of passivity and relaxation is increased by the lack of sharp contrasts, and the centered and balanced design.

Right: In this advertisement for sailboard equipment, the designer has cleverly used blues and greens (to suggest the sea) and reds, oranges, and browns (associated with warmth, vitality, and activity) in a vivid and very active image. The impression of speed is created by the fast and simple line of the figure and the board, and the white jagged diagonal crest of the wave. The thick white typography matches the power of the white outlined figure and board. Mixing red and blue generally creates a slightly aggressive tension in a design, which has been used to good effect in this image, where the red figure advances from the blue background.

Vivid red is the color most closely associated with action, youth, and vitality. It suggests the impulsiveness and spontaneity of youth, of physical activity, dancing, sports, and gymnastics. It is therefore an appropriate color to sell goods aimed at the young, such as sports equipment, music, and soft drinks.

All colors in the "warm" section of the color wheel are highly stimulating to the appetite. Orange-red is therefore especially popular for the decor of fast-food restaurants, to encourage customers to enter, order, eat and leave in reasonably rapid succession. Red implies the impatient, busy, and assertive personality: it is often the choice for fast sports cars; and in heraldry, red is symbolic of bravery and boldness. It can be used in small quantities to add life and vitality to an otherwise passive design. Red typography, say, would advance and bring life to a neutral gray or cream ground.

Left: This collection of package designs for nutritious foods for sports enthusiasts has utilized several of the well-known associations – red and brown for food (in the package for glucose and fiber foods), and blue for medicine (in the pack of vitamin and protein pills). Again, the concept of speed comes across in the diagonal bands of color, as in the rapidly outlined pastel figure and the strong italic typography of the brand name.

Combinations of Hue

Color combinations that are characteristically most re-laxing and passive are located in the "cool" sector of the color wheel, extending from the mature mid-greens of natural foliage through the cool sea greens and blues to the deep shadowy blue-violets.

In graphic design terms, passivity is suggested when a few selected hues, close together on the color wheel, are harmonized with gray or set against a neutral ground. Strident or dazzling contrasts have the opposite effect. Calmness can be suggested by monochromatic color schemes featuring lighter and darker variations of a single hue, or of variations of a hue combined with neutral grays, although very muted colors are rarely memorable.

There are no hard-and-fast rules, but feelings of passivity seem to be induced whenever the colors in a design succeed in matching the observer or customer's interior mood.

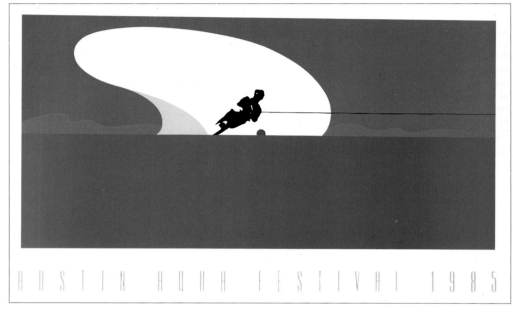

Above: This subtle but very strong poster design for the Austin Aqua Festival is the result of some fascinating contrasts. The cool blues and greens of the sea, sky, and land create a passive background for the tension of the small black diagonal water-skiing figure, silhouetted against the opposing diagonal of the billowing white wave shape. The tiny red buoy to the right of the figure helps to focus attention on it, and the tension of the contrasting diagonals creates the impression of a swiftly moving figure in a calm, relaxing background.

Right: These colors are often associated with vibrant, lively images, but the low saturations, subtle combinations of hue, and patchworked texture creates a low-key and stable impression. The busy shapes, although somewhat busy, are carefully balanced and the typography is small and delicate, adding to the atmosphere of reassurance.

HEAT FROM THE HEART

For that one time when you can use some help with your heating expenses. Your neighbors have already set up a nest egg for this emergency. The Community Heating Fund. For more information, call your local American Red Cross chapter at this number.

COLOR VARIATIONS

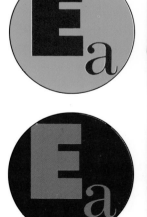

Pastel and dark-toned, more saturated colors – combined without too much contrast – are usually perceived as passive. Passive combinations imply: Thoughtfulness, moderation.

Right: This design for a pack of children's vitamins makes good use of contrasting blues and oranges to bring life and energy – suitably enough – to the package design. Set on a white background, the saturated colors sing out, and the typography also stands out well. The lack of black in the design keeps it lively and airy, as does the irregular typography in the words "Children's Vitamins."

Sanatogen ®
CHILDREN'S
VITAMINS
IN FIVE
FRUITY FLAVOURS

FOR TODAY'S LIFESTYLE

The active colors are typically centered on the red, orange-red, and orange-yellow segments of the color wheel, extending through the garnet reds, vermilion and poppy red to chrome orange and tangerine, cadmium orange and chrome yellow deep.

The liveliness of the active hues can be increased further by combining each with its complementary color, located diagonally opposite on the color wheel: red against green, orange against blue, and yellow against violet.

In particular, ultramarine blue also possesses an advancing assertiveness, while the most retiring and peaceful impressions are given by mid-to-cool greens and grays. The individual power, along with the legibility, of any single hue, is generally enhanced when isolated against a black ground.

COLOR VARIATIONS

Vivid, fully saturated colors create an active impression, particularly in striking contrasts. Active combinations imply: Youth, fun, energy.

Right: This poster (one of a series) advertising the Berlin Jazz Festival in 1989 conveys a feeling of activity, rebelliousness and inventiveness with its strongly contrasting colors and its myriad pattern of irregular shapes, created from a collage of cut-out paper. The barely legible wording has been incorporated into the shapes in an almost riddle-like manner, breaking the rules of design somewhat in the same way that jazz breaks the rules of music.

Tone and Saturation

Combinations of colors appear at their most passive when a design possesses no strong contrasts of tone and saturation. Passivity may be reinforced firstly by selecting a single, preferably cool hue and mixing with it various amounts of white, gray or black in order to grade the hue through a series of subtle steps from lighter to darker and/or from vivid to dull.

A reliably passive and stable balance of tonal contrasts is ideally expressed by the usual organization of colors in nature: that is, with dark-toned colors at the base, blending to medium-toned colors at the horizon or eye-level, to light, pastel or pale-toned colors at the top.

To create an impression of passivity, color saturation should be low and subdued, with small amounts of gray added to each selected hue to obtain a series of rich but quietly subtle colors, such as bleached denim, steel blue, smoke blue, aquamarine, lavender, and pewter.

Above: Although this design (for the front and back covers of a publisher's catalog) is very active in style, with a fast, black, single line, the use of strong, highly saturated colors on the front, and pale-toned, lightly saturated colors on the back creates a very different impression, showing how color choices can enhance or restrain the graphic elements of the design.

Left: This packaging design for Maseta coffee produces a curiously passive and restful image, both from the highly saturated dark blue background, and from the pale-toned central image of the cup, along with the combination of the squarely rooted, arch-shaped panel, and the heavy white type beneath its base. The blue and gold combination suggests the coffee is a quality item, and the feeling of calmness inspired by the package design is intended to convey the impression that drinking coffee is relaxing.

COLOR VARIATIONS

Dark tone | Mid tone | Light tone

Full saturation | Mid saturation | Low saturation

Top: Darker tones tend to look more passive than pale ones, because they recede more into the background.

Above: The lower the saturation, the more passive the color.

Since our color vision is most sensitive to yellow light and least sensitive to violet, the colors of the color wheel possess an in-built tonality, with yellow appearing simultaneously light-toned at full saturation and violet appearing much darker when fully saturated.

In printed graphics, the most saturated colors are the process primary colors: magenta, yellow, and cyan, and any combination of these at 100 percent strength will guarantee an active impression. Orange obtained by mixing yellow and magenta (in the four-color printing process) will not appear as saturated as a pre-mixed orange ink.

Far more aggressive at catching our attention than either paints or printing inks are the colors emitted by bright city lights – such as the red neon tubes, yellow sodium vapor, and green argon lamps of central city areas such as Times Square in New York, or Piccadilly Circus in London.

Left: This undeniably forceful design for a chain of cycle stores is achieved through strong, simple graphics and a limited palette of strongly contrasting but highly saturated colors. The freewheeling logo, with speed lines working in parallel to create a bold "F," embodies the best characteristics of good logo design – memorability, clarity and logic.

COLOR VARIATIONS

Dark tone

Mid tone

Light tone

Full saturation

Mid saturation

Low saturation

Above: This package design for a healthy cereal bar breaks the mold by departing from the tradition of using soft "natural" colors to identify wholesome foods. The brilliant yellow gives the package instant shelf "stand out," with a strong, active feel. The healthy element is confined mainly to the logo, with the hand and the ear of wheat in a traditional engraving-style illustration.

Shapes and Edges

A passive form is one that has found its level and equilibrium. It appears to have settled down, and is wholly at rest. Stability in a design is promoted by shapes that are bottom-heavy, such as the triangle, pediment, or semi-circular arch, which are often used in designs where traditional values are being expressed.

The passive is reinforced by designs which stress a straight horizontal base in combination with regular curves and simple symmetrical forms.

There are various techniques the designer can use to enhance the passive element of a design, by softening the edges and the contours between colors, and by applying color with an airbrush or in watercolor washes. Allowing one color to bleed into another also helps to make the distinctions less sharp, and therefore more passive. Quiet, cool colors help to emphasize passive shapes, and gentle gradations of color and blurred edges also increase the passive element.

Below: This sophisticated but very passive design for an exclusive toilet water package has a strong horizontal bias with its even black and white striped background, broken only by the flashes of primary color on the left, and the jagged black and white, arch-shape cutting across it.

Right: This screen-printed poster for a students' library conveys a terse message in a traditionally inspired design. Using many of the design devices of the 19th- and turn-of-the-century eras, along with the passive connotations of the arch shape, it manages to convey the impression of respectability and reflection suitable for a library, while putting over the message in unequivocal terms.

COLOR VARIATIONS

The forms – the shapes and edges – that confine different colors affect our perception of them. The passive is suggested by:
- soft-edged shapes
- emphasis on horizontal elements in the design
- rounded shapes

Right: A poster for a museum exhibit on "The Grand Game of Baseball" makes good use of contrast to convey an impression of the movement and activity involved in the game itself, with the academic nature of the exhibit. The vivid, swirling orange line tracing the path of the ball, the strong, curved shape of the figure and the contrasts of tone and color bring life and movement to the design, while the soft gray-green background creates a more stable and passive background.

Below right: Another poster in the series for the Berlin Jazz Festival again makes use of fragmented, disparate and asymmetric shapes to create the vibrant atmosphere of the music itself. The small, white highlights add to the liveliness of the shapes, while the tonal contrast creates a very active impression as the figures advance and recede.

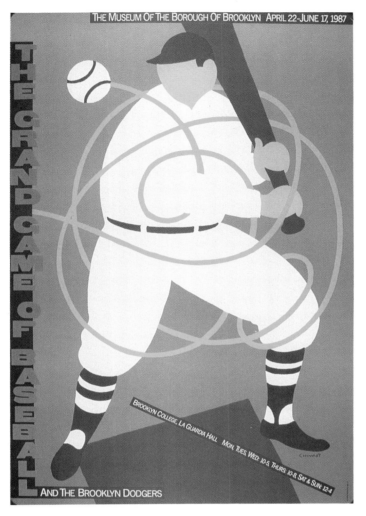

Intersecting or interwoven linear shapes, gestural swirls and curves, along with strong diagonals, all add movement to the design, and therefore help to give it an active feel.

Where the whole design is a combination of fragmented forms with no feature on which the eye can rest, the active impact is even stronger. Other active shapes are zigzags or irregular, jazzy forms that appear to float and flicker on the page.

Vivid colors and strong contrasts tend to increase the active impact. Hard-edged shapes increase the sense of movement, and, in photography, ensuring there are no shadows helps to increase the strong, active impact of the picture.

COLOR VARIATIONS

The forms – the shapes and edges – that confine different colors affect our perception of them. The active is suggested by:
- hard-edged shapes
- emphasis on diagonal elements in the design
- jagged shapes

Size and Proportion

A feeling of passivity is achieved by designs in which all the contributing colors, shapes, and proportions appear to lock together and are at rest. This is best achieved by allowing one single feature at the base of the design to dominate the others, so that it presents itself unambiguously as the center of attention.

The passive is suggested by designs with a low center of gravity, such as when type is concentrated at the base of a poster, advertisement, or package, or a label is placed low down on a container. To induce a passive feeling in a small package, it pays to use either a few varieties of shape, or else to use different sizes of a single shape,

preferably those which emphasize the horizontal element of the design. When reading lines of type, the eye is at its most relaxed when reading in the usual way, ie horizontally from left to right.

Below: This low-key, restrained and dignified design was created to sell the image of Britain's Society of Designers. Large expanses of a single color – in this case gray – help to induce a passive and reflective response from the observer, and even the strong orange of the lettering on the left-hand side fails to assert itself because it is tonally similar to the gray background. The column of white type stands out clearly from the background, balancing the deep orange-red of the left-hand side of the design.

Above: This shopping bag design for Urken Supply, a hardware store, although in strong active colors, nevertheless produces an overall passive effect, by virtue of the large type at the base of the bag, and the smallness of the vivid house illustration set in its brilliant white background. Limiting the color palette, in this case to two colors plus white, helps to create a more passive feeling.

COLOR VARIATIONS

How a color is perceived is determined by the colors that surround it, and partly by the size and proportion of the colors relative to each other. Differing proportions have been used here to show some of the effects that can be achieved as a result.

Normal perceptions of scale are based on the experience that objects appear larger when close and smaller when distant, so one way of conveying a feeling of activity in graphics is to combine images with contradictory information about size and scale.

Movement and activity is implied in a design when a sequence of interlocking forms succeeds in leading the eye relatively smoothly from one part of the design to another. The conventional tactic is to lead the viewer from the top to the base of the design, but other equally valid forms may encourage the eye to explore the perimeter of a design or to move from the edge to the center.

As a rule, regular geometric figures such as the circle and square can be made more active by distorting their proportions. The oval or ellipse appears more dynamic than the circle, and the rectangle, with the vertical dimension longer than the horizontal, more dynamic than the square. Such proportions can be enhanced by creating a design that is top-heavy, giving the impression that it is about to tilt or topple over.

Above: The background red was chosen for this cover of Network Scotland's annual report to give a lively and vibrant impression, befitting the company's work in communication. The blue and gray additions echo the colors of the company logo, and the various dropped-in images on the cover were inspired by communication-based themes.

COLOR VARIATIONS

How a color is perceived is determined by the colors that surround it, and partly by the size and proportion of the colors relative to each other. Differing proportions have been used here to show some of the effects that can be achieved as a result.

Above: Designs for a logo, clothes tag, and bags for a young fashion label for the Italian supermarket chain, Coin. The deeply saturated, strong colors, in a motif based on tick-tack-toe, are both eye-catching, exciting and stylish. The contrasts of shape and color, in the forms of the circles and crosses, give a dynamic force to the squares, which might otherwise appear too passive, while also serving to underscore the forms of the letters in the brand name, Exi-ozi (a children's pet name for tick-tack-toe).

Pattern and Texture

Passive patterns tend to be those that are quiet, unfussy, and orderly. Selected motifs are ideally soft, flat-bottomed, and at rest. Although regularity of pattern can induce a feeling of calm predictability and restfulness, a repeating pattern that refuses to allow the eye to rest on any particular feature can appear overactive. On balance, a pattern of simple and regular straight-edged shapes possessing a clear point of focus induces the greatest feeling of passivity.

Background and foreground ambiguity is best rejected in favor of uneventful or restful grounds that clearly emphasize foreground features.

For certain applications an absence of texture is most passive and tranquil. Alternatively, quietly camouflaged patterns and textures can be selected in combination with subtly textured edges, softening or dissolving the boundaries between one color and design element and another.

Above: A sophisticated and very laid back design for a range of particularly hi-tec computer software breaks the usual mold of severe geometric shapes, opting instead for a monochromatic, but tonally varied, design that repeats the triangle shape of the logo. The muted, overall patterning creates the impression of a landscape stretching to infinity, a metaphor possibly for the nature of the software.

Right: This Japanese plastic shopping bag design uses minimal color and pattern to create a simple, delicate, yet striking image. The soft elliptical central shape and the fading edge of the image in broken dots, like a printer's screen, coupled with the small but slender typography combines to create a passive but elegant impression.

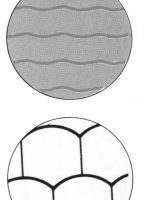

Passive patterns tend to be small, even, horizontal, and repetitive, with a limited contrast of colors – or maybe even self-colored – and lightly textured.

Patterns of similar or identical elements organized as regularly spaced grids give the impression of restlessness as the viewer has no single dominant feature on which the eye can rest. Such patterns can be effective in promoting active events, like sports, gymnastics, or dancing.

Sources for such grids include the "Op Art" of the 1960s, in which dazzling color combinations were often reinforced by interactive foreground and background shapes.

Hand-drawn or hand-painted textures also promote the feeling of activity by using thin, nervous lines, or rapidly brushed or spattered paintwork. Such animated combinations of color and form are useful for giving the impression of fun, light-heartedness, and youth, and are often used to advertise pop concerts, album covers or candy wrappers. Take care when designing graphics that are to be seen from a distance, as small areas of vivid color side by side may neutralize or cancel each other out.

Above: A brochure design for a promotional dinner to celebrate Melbourne's candidature for the 1996 Olympics. The dynamic running figures are made even more vibrant by the use of cutouts and decoration in paint-splashing techiques suggestive of Jackson Pollock.

Below: Designs for packaging for a range of icecream toppings use an unusual color combination for food (black and psychedelic pinks, yellows and blues) along with vivid patterns like candy sprinkles. The image created is one of fun, good humor and enjoyment, enhanced by the large lettering, the colloquial brand name, and the exclamation point.

COLOR VARIATIONS

Active patterns tend to be created from jagged, diagonal, jazzy shapes, with strong contrasts and vigorous, uneven lines.

FEMININE

Femininity in design can take several forms, but most often it is represented by soft, rounded, natural forms, and colors that can be bright but never strident. Contrasts used are slightly muted – blue with silver, or pale green with pink – and the images tend to draw their inspiration from nature – foliage, fruit, and flower forms being particularly popular.

Pattern and texture play a significant part in promoting a feeling of femininity, with matte surfaces, flowing typography, and rich surface patterning all contributing to a softer atmosphere. Use of toning colors for typography, rather than hard black, tends to give any design a softer, more feminine focus, and brown and blue inks are commonly used in designs with a feminine bias.

fertile

gentle

delicate

subjective

practical

rounded

modest

motherly

central

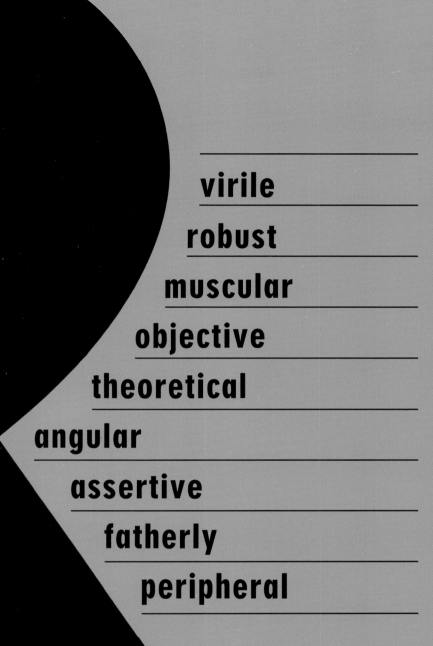

virile

robust

muscular

objective

theoretical

angular

assertive

fatherly

peripheral

Although the barriers between the genders are being broken down, and women and men can now feel comfortable doing jobs that were almost unthinkable only a generation ago, the definitions of, and the concepts conjured up by, the terms "masculine" and "feminine" still apply.

A graphic designer may well be asked to come up with a strongly "masculine" design. This will almost inevitably carry connotations of strength and boldness, using highly saturated colors, sharp edges, and possibly abstract images. The colors usually associated with "masculine" design are those of the old-time smoking room or club tie colors – the dark reds, greens, browns, and navy blues.

Hard, shiny metallic surfaces, high-gloss papers, and sanserif bold typefaces all have a strong masculine feel, as do emphatic tonal contrasts.

MASCULINE

Color Associations

Although we should avoid reinforcing outdated or limited preconceptions about femaleness, a commercial market does exist that is directed specifically at female preferences. Traditional associations combine sophistication with practicality and the down-to-earth with the alluring. Colors perceived as feminine are the greens of foliage, the golds, pinks, and mauves of flowers, and the pale pastel tints of all hues. They tend to be associated with the promotion of beauty products such as perfumes and cosmetics, soaps and shampoos, skincare products, lotions, and talcum powders, along with specialty goods and foods manufactured for babies and toddlers.

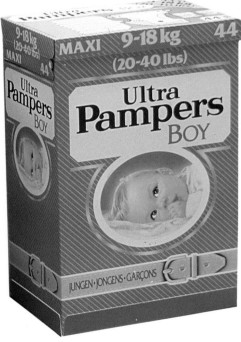

Above: A beauty notebook deploys some of the classic concepts of feminine-oriented design and color combinations to convey a message of subtlety, sophistication, and modernity for a young, female clientele. The soft pastel shades and marbled endpapers contrast with the stylized modern logo and the use of black to convey the sense of contrast that now represents modern femininity – soft-centered but businesslike.

Left: Blue for boys and pink for girls may be a cliché, but it works well for these packages of his and hers babies' diapers, which can be sorted visually at some distance by the customer in a hurry. Baby products are generally given a traditional and practical treatment, and these diaper packages are no exception.

Left: The logo for Talbot cars is unequivocally masculine, using a strong, aggressive contrast of red and blue, in firm, bold shapes, plain sans serif lettering, made even more forceful by the use of shadowing on the "T" logo, which gives it an almost three-dimensional effect.

Conveying an image of masculinity is best achieved with strong and easily identifiable colors, notably red, deep brown, deep blue, and silver. Masculine colors are usually deemed appropriate for promoting industrial goods, including building materials, goods associated with machinery, transportation, and automobiles, sports events (such as ball games and boxing matches), and various brands of beer, whiskey and cigarette.

Vivid orange-red, symbolic of Mars, the Roman god of war, and once popular for military uniforms, possesses a strength and attention-catching power unmatched among all other hues, especially when set against deep navy blue or black. Whereas black is favored by men for gifts they buy women, red is a consistently popular choice in gifts that women buy for men.

In design history, masculinity can best be identified with the sober coloring and logical structure of the Victorian Arts and Crafts movement and later with the severity of the Bauhaus style in the 1920s and '30s.

Sharp contrasts tend to have a more masculine feel, such as orange and black, blue with yellow, and red with white.

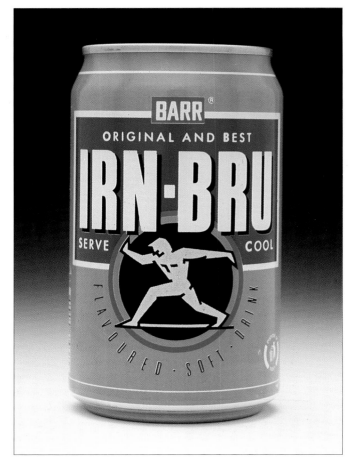

Right: This redesign for an Irn-Bru soft drink can helped to boost sales considerably, by creating a strong, sporting and modern image that retained the existing children's market, but appealed to adults too. The unusual and striking contrast of orange and blue, the vigorous running figure, and the clear, bold brand name looks both modern, invigorating and clean. Although the color combination is more masculine than feminine, the package has an almost androgynous appeal.

Combinations of Hue

Color selections that best represent femininity embody the twin qualities of strength and softness. In general, colors most associated with femininity are those that occur in nature – leaf greens, and petal mauves and pinks, often in subtly blending combinations rather than sharper contrasts.

A more modern and rather tougher image of feminine sensuality might be expressed in a monochromatic scheme of black and silvery gray, with pinky-red highlights. Great care needs to be taken to avoid combinations that have become so over-used that they are now a design cliché. As far as color schemes for products related to women's fashions and cosmetics are concerned, popular fashion colors can be a more dominant force, changing with remarkable rapidity.

Left: This range of award-winning Japanese cosmetic designs combine feminine delicacy with a clear, modern image. The unusual choice of smooth, bright, acid colors for the decoration on the packs has been offset by the textured matte gray ground and the thinness of the line, while the embossed brand name adds a touch of class.

Left: These hoisery packs utilize the concepts traditionally associated with feminine appeal: toning pastel colors, delicate patterning and soft focus photography all contribute to a romantic and dreamy image.

COLOR VARIATIONS

Pastel combinations of bright flashes of color on a dark ground are perceived as feminine. Feminine combinations imply: Sensitivity with strength.

Right: This black, gold, and red combination is one frequently chosen to convey an image of masculinity with a touch of class, emphasized by the traditional style of the typography and the bottle design. Red implies strength, black implies style and smoothness, and gold implies luxury.

C olor combinations generally regarded as having masculine connotations are those which are bold, unambiguous, substantial, and assertive, mainly to be found on the red/blue axis, with deep reds, ochers, russets, tans, and rich browns predominating, often complemented by deep strong blues, like Prussian, royal, cobalt and Delft.

In many ways the brightly colored, strongly contrasting bands of color in the flags of heraldic tournaments live on in the choice of masculine-oriented color schemes. In heraldry, to ensure legibility, the colors were never placed edge to edge but were outlined with white, silver, gold, or black. This functional separation of color is repeated today in many company logos and corporate images, giving the impression of boldness combined with a measure of sophistication.

Left: This advertisement for running shoes puts strong contrasts of color to good use. The green background to the runner pushes the figure forward, while the bright red background to the shoe stops him in his tracks. The blue and yellow combination of the shoe zings out from the red ground, and the combination of the large, no-nonsense typography with the vivid contrasts of primary colors convey the image of energy, strength, and performance.

COLOR VARIATIONS

Strong contrasts of color and deep-toned earthy combinations are often used to indicate masculinity. Masculine combinations imply: Boldness, assertiveness.

Right: These batteries are equally plain and no-nonsense, making use of strong color contrasts, shiny surfaces, and clear lettering to convey a feeling of strength and durabilty. Hard-edged, tough, and unequivocal, the pack design is simple but forceful.

Tone and Saturation

Although it is currently fashionable to play down differences between female and male, certain products are undoubtedly aimed exclusively at one or other category.

Pale-toned, desaturated colors are usually seen as appealing most to feminine sensitivity, but color preferences do vary with age for both sexes. Today's young women, less home-based and more self-confident than their mothers, are often more drawn to deeper saturations and brighter colors.

By and large harsh contrasts are best avoided if a product is to have a feminine appeal. Type tends to work best in toning but darker shades than those used in the design, so that the contrast is more muted and less aggressive than, say, black might be.

Above: Penhaligon's collection of toilet waters are light, floral, and feminine. The packaging was designed to put across this message, and to capitalize on the traditional English nature of the company – established for more than 100 years. Pale pastel colors, floral imagery, pink ribbon and gold lettering all help to transmit a feminine, luxurious, and traditional image.

Above: An annual report for Britain's Birth Defect Study Group has used very light saturation and pale tones to create a design for a sensitive topic. The light and spacious monochromatic design is delicate yet authoritative, the photography deliberately soft-focused and gentle.

COLOR VARIATIONS

Dark tone

Mid tone

Light tone

Full saturation

Mid saturation

Low saturation

Top: For large areas of color, paler tones generally seem more feminine than darker tones.

Above: Higher saturations are often used to indicate femininity in small areas only, contrasted with a dark ground.

While the female preference in shades of red may well be for the more unsaturated tints, the male preference tends to be for the deeper shades – the wine reds, maroons, and reddish earthy browns. The deeper saturations of blue – the navy blues – are symbolic of masculine order, reliability, and authority.

If you are overprinting type on these darker toned colors, you will need to think in terms of sharp contrasts, maybe reversing the type in a paler toned color.

Below: An equally uncompromising approach has been used for this poster for a power farming exhibition. The style has the strong graphic quality of the hand-printed German posters of the 1930s, with a similarly bold color palette of black, red, and buff. Deep shadowing and strong tonal contrasts give the poster great legibility, while the strong sweeping diagonals contribute a sense of movement and power.

Above: This unpublished poster for Nintendo computer games has utilized a strong, curiously period image for a very modern product. The hard, outlined edge, and strong tonal contrasts, with the muscular, athletic figure, convey the unmistakable impression of tough masculinity.

COLOR VARIATIONS

Dark tone   Mid tone   Light tone

Full saturation   Mid saturation   Low saturation

Top: Only the dark tones are perceived as masculine, as they imply stength and resolve.

Above: More fully saturated colors can be used to imply masculinity if darker toned. The lighter tones are too jazzy.

Shapes and Edges

Our memory of the exact shapes and colors of objects is generally surprisingly poor. For most purposes, it is enough to remember for example that a face is round or square, although no face is truly round or square. Importantly it is to such simplified memories that the designer must appeal. Physically the female form tends to be more rounded and less angular than that of the male, and images or products which exaggerate roundness, coupled with softness of outline, will emphasize the feminine aspect. References or allusions to the female form are powerful symbols in the design of packages that have a specifically feminine connotation.

The more representational natural shapes, such as the delicate outlines of petals and leaves, have long since been associated with feminine products and packaging in design and decoration. In their most sophisticated form, these traits are characterized by long, elegant shapes with softly shadowed or out-of-focus edges.

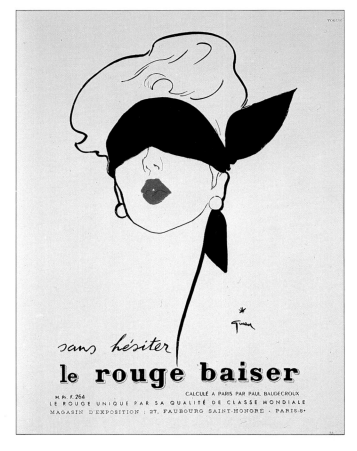

Left: This classic poster for lipstick takes a definitely more sexual approach to femininity. The contrasting black and red are more often used to promote the concept of masculinity, but when combined, as here, with a delicate, sensuous line, and forming a very small proportion of the whole design, they take on a distinctly different meaning to create an image of sophistication, worldiness, and sexuality.

Above: Softly curving outlines, Victorian-style typography, and delicate color combinations give this corporate logo and stone-front design the intimacy and appeal of a lady's boudoir. Undeniably feminine and slightly mysterious, the style is very much in keeping with the concept of the store and the nature of the product – in this case a lingerie range.

COLOR VARIATIONS

The forms – the shapes and edges – that confine different colors affect our perception of them. Femininity is suggested by:

- rounded, organic shapes
- emphasis on horizontal elements in the design
- soft curves
- toning typography

Above: This motor oil can has all the hallmarks of strong masculine design. Sturdy, square, and firmly based, with its large, easy-to-grip ribbed handle, it combines a sophisticated color combination with simple, bold and straightforward typography and a strong sense of practicality. Black and gold are commonly used to convey masculinity, strength and quality.

Below: In the appropriate armed forces colors of blue and green, this poster for London's Imperial War Museum is sharp, spare, and unequivocal. The searchlight shapes crisscrossing the horizontal barbed wire clearly communicate the message of war, while linking the typography at the top and bottom of the design. The jagged, almost raw contrast of hard-edged shapes conveys the brutal nature of war and makes a graphic, arresting image.

In general, solidity and square-ness typify the strength, stability, and muscularity often associated with male characteristics. Regular geometric forms, straight edges, and sharp edges are seen as typically masculine. In letter forms, bold, geometrical sanserif faces have a strong masculine feel.

Masculine patterns tend to be those of repeated combinations of intersecting vertical, horizontal, and diagonal lines, in abstract, linear, or geometric shapes.

COLOR VARIATIONS

The forms – the shapes and edges – that confine different colors affect our perception of them. Masculinity is suggested by:
square, geometric shapes
- emphasis on the vertical in the design
- hard-edged angles
- bold sanserif type

Size and Proportion

In the packaging and promoting of products aimed at the female purchaser, it is often the small, the slender, and the delicately proportioned that appeal to feminine taste. Softly rounded forms in sympathetic textured materials that are warm to the touch are considered to have more feminine appeal than hard-edged ones with glossy, smooth surfaces.

On a practical level, products that are frequently used by women and that need to be regularly handled – whether bottles of shampoo and bath oil, or larger containers for detergents or cleaning products – need to be designed in sizes and proportions that can be manipulated easily by the smaller female hand.

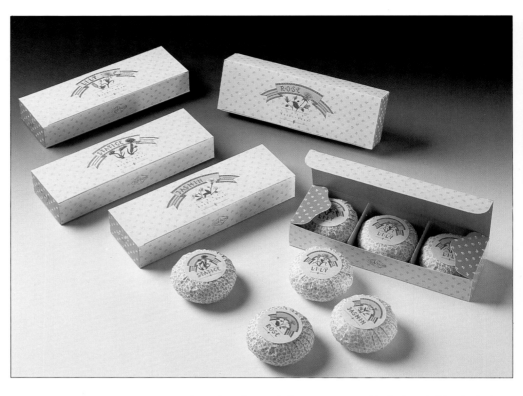

Above: This collection of gift soaps draws on a number of typically feminine design concepts to create an atmosphere of delicacy and exclusivity. The smallness of the central image, with its fine botanical drawing, looks refined and sensitive, and the lack of contrasts, coupled with the pastel color combination, produces a muted, low-key, and sophisicated design.

Above: Many of the products aimed at the feminine hygiene market are packaged in a low-key style, but here good use has been made of traditionally feminine pastel colors that are given "punch" by the large, bold typography and the use of toning colors on the packs. The circle (of toning color) is widely perceived as a feminine shape.

COLOR VARIATIONS

How a color is perceived is determined by the colors that surround it, and partly by the size and proportion of the colors relative to each other. Differing proportions have been used here to show some of the effects that can be achieved as a result.

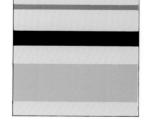

The male typically appears squarer and larger in scale than the female. In the image of the masculine body there is a greater suggestion of the monumental, the sculptural, or architectural, most obviously exhibited by the disciplined regularity of the classical. Products designed to appeal to the masculine purchaser tend to be generous in proportion, simple and unfussy, hard-edged, weighty, and substantial.

The advancing and somewhat aggressive nature of the masculine can be suggested by solid forms in relief, such as the clearly defined shapes of chunky Egyptian letterforms which are boldly outlined or shadowed.

While emphasis on horizontal divisions of a design area tends to evoke the placid or feminine, vertical divisions are more suggestive of the masculine. Repeated vertical divisions tend to group themselves and appear as advancing figures against receding grounds.

Above: This package for paper tissues has used abstract, jagged shapes in vivid, contrasting colors to create an image that is clean, bold and masculine, as befits the message that the tissues are "extra strong."

Below: An unusual hexagonal package shape and a brand name that is more appropriate to automobile-industry product have been used to draw attention to an instant energy reviver for athletes. Although intended to

appeal to sportsmen and women, the package is clearly masculine in approach and design, with its bold typography, flashes of highly saturated yellow and red' and its gray background.

COLOR VARIATIONS

How a color is perceived is determined by the colors that surround it, and partly by the size and proportion of the colors relative to each other. Differing proportions have been used here to show some of the effects that can be achieved as a result.

Pattern and Texture

Patterns conventionally associated with the feminine are dominated by long, flowing lines, scrolls, bows, frills, intricate baroque decorations, and the interwoven stems of plants such as the honeysuckle, vine, or rose.

Advertisements for women's fashion and textiles often emphasize the delicacy of silken textures, sufficiently soft, smooth, and desirable to be worn next to the skin. Other appropriate patterns and textures are those traditionally created by the lacemaker, seamstress, or embroiderer.

The rounded forms of calligraphy or handwritten signatures are often used to add a feminine touch to package designs for perfumes, hair products, special-ty baked foods, and numerous lines of fashionable goods. Of graphic techniques, it is the soft-edged and translucent quality of watercolors or the sketchy image of colored pencils, which most appropriately suggest the feminine. In photography, grainy textures and soft-focus shots, together with bleached colors, have a strong feminine appeal.

Below: A floral theme, has been used for this range of personal care products. The voluptuous white lilies, outlined in silver, have an almost Art Deco feel, and although done in pastels, this design creates a much bolder impression than the one above, mainly as a result of its emphasis on form as well as pattern.

Above: This gift box has utilized watercolors in a subtle overall floral image to create an integrated package design (the two packs of soap together create a single image). The light brushwork, the use of pastel colors – in this case in green, cream, and gold – with natural associations help to create the feeling of a very pure and essentially feminine product.

COLOR VARIATIONS

Feminine patterns are usually flowing scroll-like or floral forms, often evenly patterned, and without strong contrasts of form or color.

Right: Irregular forms and abstract patterns in asymmetric shapes and in contrasting rather than toning colors create a distinctly masculine impression in this section opener for the Next Directory mail-order catalog. The color associations of blue with strength and black with sophistication underscore the theme of a tough, masculine, modern outlook.

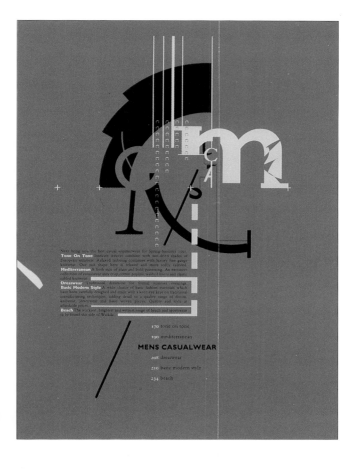

P atterns associated with the masculine tend to be bold, simple, and geometric, such as repeated vertical lines or simple, unadorned grids and frets. Emphasis is typically on the orderly and the unfussy, with perhaps large blocks of solid color, strong contrasts of tone, and dominant black typography – such as black on a signal red ground.

As far as graphics are concerned, the various forms of functional design associated with the early Constructivist and Bauhaus movements are more obviously masculine in tone and saturation. The masculine textures tend to be Spartan, tough, hardwearing, and plain. From black leather to bleached denim, the emphasis is on hard, lasting surfaces.

In photography, sharp contrasts in black and white with a high-gloss surface have the punch and impact associated with the masculine.

COLOR VARIATIONS

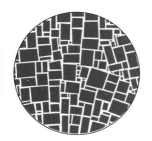

Masculine patterns tend to be bold, strongly contrasted, diagonal, geometric hard-edged shapes, often in diamonds, triangle or stripes, with black as a contrast.

Above: These two packages of paper tissues – mansize and extra strong – demonstrate how a broadly similar overall patterned design can be twisted to produce a very different impression. The gray, red, and black abstract shapes convey a definitely masculine impression for the mansize tissues, while the design for the extra strong ones (intended to appeal to both sexes) uses more rounded forms and the association of blue with strength.

NATURAL

The term "natural" inevitably conjures up images of the rural landscape – the soft blues, grays, greens, and ochers of the hills and fields. These images, along with their colors, are widely used in a range of design contexts to evoke a nostalgia for the simplicity and charm of nature.

The unadulterated colors of natural pigments – the cobalts, ochers, and umbers – are a powerful reminder of a pre-industrial age when a natural rather than a human-made order predominated.

Softly focused, twining images, often with fruit, flowers, and leaves, are widely used in packaging products associated with nature – healthy breakfast cereals, good quality jams and conserves, natural toiletries and cosmetics.

genuine

instinctive

organic

rural

spontaneous

wholesome

grown

improvised

ingenuous

imitation
learned
geometric
urban
rehearsed
synthetic
manufactured
orchestrated
contrived

The bright acidity of the printer's primary colors – yellow, cyan, magenta – is obviously and immediately chemical and artificial in origin. Bright, sharp contrasts, hard edges and outlines, and punchy typography all grab attention. Using these sharp contrasts and unsubtle colors presents a brash modern idiom, far removed from the gentle combinations commonly associated with nature.

Equally artificial are strong contrasts of light and dark, associated with the glare of fluorescent lighting and its lurid contrasts. Geometric designs represent the artificiality and precision molding of machine-made objects. Textures are hard, reflective, and glossy, like the smooth-sprayed surfaces of metal and enamel.

ARTIFICIAL

Color Associations

The most obvious impressions that natural color call to mind are those of the surrounding landscape. For certain products, seasonal considerations are an important factor in their packaging and promotion. Summer may be imagined as a patchwork of browns, greens, and yellows illuminated by golden sunlight, and bounded by the shadowy blue-greens of deep water. Such images of nature are often exploited in the packaging and sales of wholemeal and natural grains, breakfast cereals, nuts, seeds, fresh or frozen fruit and vegetables, and poultry.

Nature the provider also gives the designer numerous traditional paint and ink pigments, such as rusty iron oxides – familiar as raw umber, raw sienna, and Indian red – which can be used to good effect to create a natural impression.

Top: The naturalistic color in this advertisement is color-enhanced, evoking the idea of a back-to-the-land lifestyle and exposure to the elements. The practicality of the product – waterproof shoes – gains a definite and attractively presented context. The whole image is pure and uncomplicated in its design, in keeping with the message.

Above: Autumnal, earthy hues and golden light are emphasized in this image, in accord with the date of the advertised marathon. The natural parchment color of the background and rich brown of the type discreetly relate to the pictorial color themes.

Right: Modern printing colors, heightened and intensified, are presented in tonal gradations that make the image appear illuminated, adding to the sense of artificiality. The layering of the image is associated with design devices provided by computer graphic facilities. This is, in all respects, a design from a technological age.

Below: Each can color is a typically pure, artificial hue, associated more with the general idea of a fun drink than with individual flavors. The process of printing colors over white makes them especially vivid. This packaging is deliberately brash and eye-catching, with a fresh, young appeal.

A large number of the colors used nowadays for paints and printing inks are artificial in origin, synthesized from organic (mostly coal-tar) dyestuffs. Common examples include quinacridone magenta, azo yellow, and phthalocyanine (or cyan) blue, which make up the printer's primaries. At their most garish they are reminiscent of cheap plastic toys or picnic cups and saucers – objects which are colorful and attractive but ephemeral and disposable.

Artificial colors are well suited to the packaging of soft drinks, children's games and toys, teenage summer clothes, and for items such as playground jungle gyms in which the vivid colors of plastics promote positive associations of fun and enjoyment. Such colors can often be exploited in comics and pop music album covers, as well as cheaply printed fliers for festivals and rock concerts.

Artificial colors tend to be brash, stimulating, unsubtle, and eye-catching. As highlights or points of focus in a design, they are ideal for grabbing our attention and reviving concentration, but can become tiring if made to command our gaze over too long a period.

ARTIFICIAL

Combinations of Hue

Natural color reveals itself most spectacularly in the broad arc of the rainbow, with red above orange, yellow, green, blue, and violet, luminous against a thundery gray sky. Rainbows are memorable but rare, and the combination of colors more commonly equated with the vistas and objects of nature are centered in the top half of the color circle, ranging from leaf greens through deep fall yellows to earthy reds and browns. Such a range of colors is useful for promoting the concept of fresh fruit and vegetables and the qualities of organically grown high-fiber food, for example. Alternatively blues can be combined for the packaging and labeling of bottled mineral water.

A close examination of the surface of almost any individual natural object will prove that nature is full of surprises. Fruits, vegetables and other natural produce often place together remarkably daring contrasts of color, many of which become apparent on close examination only. The natural landscape consists almost entirely of optically blended colors in which individual color ingredients, such as red berries set against green foliage, appear blended and harmonious when viewed from a distance.

Below: Green, brown, and blue, the colors of landscape, form the basic color themes for this packaging. The wholesomeness of the product is directly evoked in the watercolor imagery of farmland, on which the dark-toned type panels are overlaid. The white typography is shadowed in yellow for extra weight.

Right: This poster makes use of obviously natural imagery in the shapes as well as the greens and golds of vegetation and the blues of the oceans to convey the message. The surreal feel to the image, and the impression of distance created by the background sum up the concept of wide horizons and infinite powers.

DOING A WORLD OF GOOD

Pigment and earth colors are often used to evoke a natural atmosphere. Natural combinations imply: Wholesomeness, tradition, reassurance.

Right: Intense "plastic" colors call to mind children's building blocks, an apt association for the image. But contrary to this first impression, the color combinations have a distinctively adult sophistication. The subtlety of the gray and mauve shades enhances the apparent brightness of the purer hues – orange, red, and green – but analysis of the particular character of each color selected from the chromatic range reveals the designer's expert command of color interactions.

Below right: The rainbow effect of stripes, colored to match the candies in this pack, sets up the problem of devising a typographic treatment that will read across the range from black to yellow. White type is only one of the possible solutions, but here it is particularly effective when given colored outlines that directly link the lettering to the background.

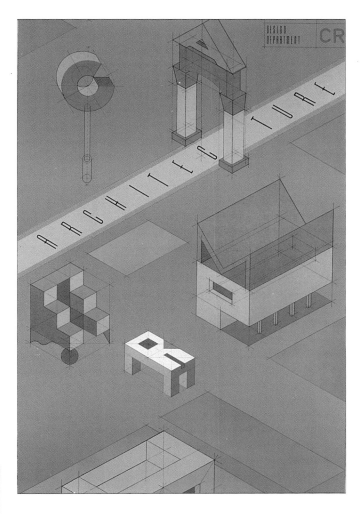

The full-strength colors of the color circle present us with bold, unsubtle contrasts that are often rather garish. Combinations of such colors, against a white, gray or black ground, are ideal for grabbing our attention and keeping us alert.

There is something particularly artificial about the printer's primaries – the magenta, cyan, and yellow – which are more reminiscent of stimulating, noisy interiors, like the playrooms and schoolrooms for the young. The artificial colors are particularly useful for selling children's goods and are also useful for situations where attention needs to be drawn and held for a short period only.

In graphic design, suitably bold type will be needed to ensure that the vividness of the colors does not dominate the design, confusing the message and preventing it from getting across.

COLOR VARIATIONS

Sharp, acid colors, combined with strong contrasts, tend to look artificial. Artifical combinatións imply: Modernity, youthfulness, fun.

Tone and Saturation

Owing to particles of dust and water vapor in the air, the colors of the landscape exhibit a natural order in which foreground colors tend to be deep in tone and warm, while those in the distance are lighter in tone and cooler in hue. This can be used to suggest expansiveness in a design, offering a "perspective" of color that invites the viewer into the depth of a pictorial or imaginary space.

Viewed from a distance, nature's colors appear muted and insubstantial, yet it is common to visualize or remember "grass green" or "sky blue" as brighter or more vivid than they actually are. The actual colors of nature tend to be suprisingly low in saturation compared to the vividness of printing inks. Buff, cream, or beige backgrounds give a "natural" feeling to graphic images, particularly when printed on textured paper. The vignetting of photographs and the use of sepia both help to create a nostalgic mood which harks back to a more "natural" era.

Right: The even tone of this design derives from the use of naturalistic colors with softened contrasts. The most vivid color element is the sunburst at the corner of the design, but although quite saturated, this is pale in tone. The gentle mood of the color treatment underlines the naturalness that is part of the product's appeal.

Below: In this design which uses yellows and green of citrus fruit with bright red and brilliant blue, the designers have successfully communicated the concept of a traditional product that is lively, youthful, and full of zest.

COLOR VARIATIONS

Dark tone

Mid tone

Light tone

Full saturation

Mid saturation

Low saturation

Top: The degree of tone makes little difference to the concept of naturalness, but the choice of hue is all-important.

Above: The very brightest saturations of even the most natural colors tend to convey a more artificial impression.

Artificiality is exhibited in high-key colors which combine overall lightness of tone with maximum saturation. They are most typically the unmixed and unsubtle colors that excite, warm, and dazzle. Such colors have a transitory, insubstantial quality, their saturation at its fullest when they are presented as thin layers of printed lithographic inks, utilizing the transparency of the ink layer in combination with the whiteness of the paper support to enhance the purity of their reflected light. Premixed inks generally achieve more saturated artificial colors.

The colors that appear most obviously artificial are the luminous fluorescent or phosphorescent paints and inks. These consist of pigments combined with crystals capable of converting invisible ultraviolet energy from the sun into visible light. They are commonly added as "optical brightening agents" to soap powders and cleansing liquids to neutralize the yellowness of natural fibers and to create a "whiter than white" wash.

Above: In brochures forming promotional material for the seasonal ranges of a textile company, photographic images of flowers have been used, but they are color-enhanced, so the saturation is more intense than it would be in nature. This linkage of the natural and artificial suggests an appropriate association with the range of materials and processes involved in textile manufacture.

Below: The structure of this design contrasts various color elements: the letterforms are in strong, warm hues; the background colors are cooler and slightly less saturated. The tonal version shows an unexpectedly high degree of contrast when the chromatic factor is eliminated. The color range is abstract, artificial, and non-associative.

COLOR VARIATIONS

Dark tone

Mid tone

Light tone

Full saturation

Mid saturation

Low saturation

Top: Both the very pale and very dark tones lose the sharpness associated with artificial colors.

Above: The highest saturations tend to look more artificial than the lower ones – the more vivid, the better.

Shapes and Edges

Natural colors evoke natural shapes, ranging from the soft curves of rolling farmland to the stark, jagged silhouettes of trees or mountain ranges against a luminous sky.

On the whole, nature's shapes are organic, individual, and full of contrasts. Compare the delicate shapes of petals and flower stems with the massive solidity of boulders or tree trunks.

Other shapes which come to mind are winding footpaths with spiky, overhanging branches, or smoothly rounded hillsides with distant contours softened by hovering blue mists.

The use of predominantly horizontal lines in a design will readily suggest the distant horizon of a landscape or seascape. In a landscape, we can visualize the soft-edged blending of one natural object with another. The shapes tend to be layered, and have torn rather than clean-cut edges.

Soft pencil, charcoal, and watercolor washes can all be used to create softly blurred effects with natural edges, rather than the sharp definitions of felt-tip pens.

Left: This image is based on a very literal interpretation of the copy line, simply using the natural shapes and colors of the subject as a background to the logo. The variety of the pebbles is eye-catching and pleasing. Such a direct graphic statement leaves open the associative possibilities that the viewer may bring to the presentation.

Above: Food packages of traditional style – solid shapes with softened contours – are made from opaque paper rather than the often preferred see-through plastic wrapper. This gives a pale ground for the type and cutout illustrations, centered in traditional style, and presented in wholesome creams and browns. All of these harmonious elements contribute to a brand image that shows the products as natural and desirable.

COLOR VARIATIONS

The forms – the shapes and edges – that confine different colors affect our perception of them. The natural is suggested by:
- organic shapes
- softly blending edges
- handmade marks and flowing forms

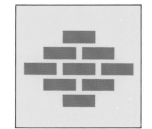

Left: Cutout shapes are a graphic device often used to evoke modern art references. Here strong process colors and hard, irregular edge qualities are combined in a dynamic, even aggressive, abstracted image.

Below: Black, red, and white is a very strong, hi-tec color combination – it has no natural equivalent. Here it is applied to a design approach that has to accommodate a number of differently shaped packages. A common feature is the dominant red initial letter wrapping over the edge of the package. The illustration of the object floating on a background of graduated tone gives a slightly surreal effect.

Common examples of artificial shapes include trademarks and logos in which, for example, a natural form, often combined with initials or lettering, has been adapted to form a stylized or geometric symbol. Unlike natural forms, machine-made shapes tend to be regular and repetitive, having been designed with precise draftsmanship and molded and manufactured with cool, sharp-edged accuracy. Artificial shapes are typically based on grids and geometric designs with vivid color added as an afterthought.

Designs combining perfectly circular, square, pointed, or rectangular shapes with hard, sharp edges look most artificial when the associated colors are those normally infused into cheap plastics or sprayed and enameled onto metallic surfaces.

COLOR VARIATIONS

The forms – the shapes and edges – that confine different colors affect our perception of them. The artificial is suggested by:
- geometric or abstract shapes
- sharp edges
- clean and straight-edged images

Size and Proportion

The proportions of natural forms are reassuringly balanced and harmonious. In general, the expansiveness of nature can be imitated by placing large and roughly textured forms in the foreground, or at the base of the design, and finer and smoother forms in the distance or at the top. Their combination then feels correctly weighted, conforming to the proportions of natural landscapes.

Though natural scenery extends horizontally from foreground to background, we have become accustomed to seeing it flatly framed in books, posters, and magazines. The main reason that such an image looks so realistic is that particular attention has been given to the relative size and scale of the objects within the picture. Though we know that the objects or figures in the image are almost always larger than they are in the picture, we accept them as lifesized because they appear correctly in scale in relation to other objects and the context in which they are shown.

Below and right: In both of these designs the image occupies a greater proportion than the type area; the main message is subservient to the visual symbol. The scale of the image immediately catches the eye and directs it down to the typography. Both make use of the object's natural colors, though not in a directly naturalistic way, and the color theme extends to the type matter. In the tree poster, the dominance of the silhouetted image means that the color becomes representative of the idea. The design of the bag can be seen to work at different scales and on different materials – the natural-colored burlap bag and the smaller Cellophane version.

PLANT

A BETTER FUTURE

Public Service

COLOR VARIATIONS

How a color is perceived is determined by the colors that surround it, and partly by the size and proportion of the colors relative to each other. Differing proportions have been used here to show some of the effects that can be achieved as a result.

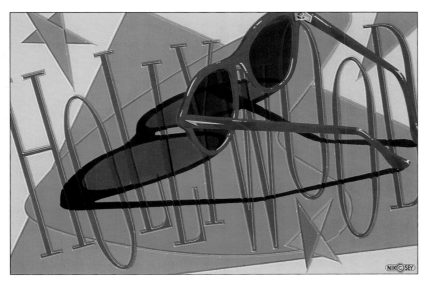

When an item is human-made, especially for mass-production, there is usually a concern for economy in the way in which individual units are combined to form a whole. Often this involves making the design conform to a predetermined grid, as occurs in graphics when the jagged-edge forms dictated by the grids of pixels on the television screen or the dot matrix structure of a computer printout interrupt or distort the flow of naturally curved lines. Using representations of such stepped and stylized shapes and letterforms can project a feeling not only of artificiality but of up-to-date technological efficiency.

Artificially bright colors can be added to a manufactured product or item in order to enhance its attractiveness, apparent sweetness, or freshness, or to make it appear "larger than life." Artificial high-key colors tend not to blend well. They jar, and often give a somewhat dazzling impression when viewed together, especially when each area covers roughly the same proportion of the surface area of a design.

COLOR VARIATIONS

How a color is perceived is determined by the colors that surround it, and partly by the size and proportion of the colors relative to each other. Differing proportions have been used here to show some of the effects that can be achieved as a result.

Top: The outlining of this shape gives the design a dynamic perspective that enhances its relative scale. The narrow neon-style typeface reads more substantially because the outline creates a three-dimensional effect. The colors seem evenly distributed within the linear design, which does not allow any solid mass of one color that might dominate, and it is this linearity that makes the name fully legible across the color range.

Above left: These colors are unashamedly artificial, creating a bold, brash, fun image. And it is the whole image that is important in conveying the message and mood, all the contributing elements being interwoven. The fine, elongated letterforms are readily decipherable but inseparable from the whole.

Pattern and Texture

Natural patterns are irregular, organic, and fragmentary, suggestive of the wildness of wide-open spaces. Such patterns often involve various forms of camouflage in which one texture blends indistinctly into others beside and around it. Nature itself provides an endless variety of plant forms, such as wheatsheaves, fruit, vegetables, flowers, leaves, and interwoven stems and vines. These can all be simplified, stylized, and repeated in designs used to sell any number of products connected with the countryside.

Useful textures for promoting and selling winter clothes, foods, and products associated with an outdoor life include representations of grasses, and woven natural fibers, such as woolen tweeds, in softly blended vegetable dyed colors.

A growing range of "natural" papers is now available to the designer, including rough recycled and handmade papers, although these have limitations in the four-color printing process, because they do not always take the inks well.

Above: The discreet, stone-like texture of this box is displayed, with its contents, on a background of real slate. The image has a cool, classical feel that is essentially timeless. The sophistication of the product is also represented in the embossed label with gold type.

Right: A vibrant pointillist impression of light on water is a clever way to bring originality to an everyday product that would more usually be sold with a simple photograph of the package's contents. As well as making an attractive pattern background to a plain label, the modern art reference is designed to appeal to an upscale clientele.

COLOR VARIATIONS

Natural patterns are often representational images from nature – leaves, stems, flowers and fruit – with a strong emphasis on texture as well as pattern.

NATURAL

On the one hand, artificiality suggests orderly and mechanical patterning in the form of a chessboard grid or the regular patterns of brickwork, tiles, and paving stones. Isometric projections and grids, drawn with great attention to detail, give a greater feel for the artificial than traditional two-point linear perspective. Alternatively, there is something unambiguously urban and artificial in both the shapes and colors of the letter forms created by the teenage spray-can graffiti artist.

The artificial typically suggests surfaces that are die-cut, molded, highly polished, and devoid of texture, such as large, flatly printed areas of color applied to smooth, machine-made surfaces. Artificial colors tend to be printed, sprayed, or stenciled. Each method possesses its own qualities which can be exploited to enhance the manufactured feel.

Above: A smooth, flat-surface quality gives full value to the individual colored shapes in this swimwear logo design. The swimmers and water are interpreted as repetitive pattern elements, printed in bright color on a black ground. This high contrast adds to the sparkle of the hues, in keeping with the subject.

COLOR VARIATIONS

Artificial patterns are smooth, streamlined and impersonal, creating a glassy, lightly patterned surface, often associated with a high-gloss finish.

Left: In this concert poster design, sharp, highly saturated acidic colors in sweeping irregular forms advance from the mottled, more muted background, creating the vibrant, energetic, and exciting image of the conductor on the podium.

ARTIFICIAL

EXCLUSIVE

Exclusive, by definition, relates to the minority. Colors associated with the exclusive tend to be subtle art shades in rich deep tones, often with a jewel-like quality.

In design terms, the exclusive is often represented by dignified, simple shapes which exploit the beauty of natural, but rare, materials, such as silk, velvet, or silver. Pattern and texture form an integral part of the design, and are usually restrained and elegant.

When colors are combined, the palette is often deliberately limited to two or three. Silver and gold lettering are often used on rich deep background colors.

refined

artful

luxurious

cultured

select

witty

self-conscious

expensive

upmarket

brash

artless

common

youthful

mass-market

funny

exhibitionist

inexpensive

downmarket

Fifty years or so ago, popular design was identified principally with cheap, mass-produced goods in shoddy materials. Since then, a growing consumer awareness of good design has encouraged a new attitude to popular design, although bright colors, easy-to-read graphics, and cheaply produced materials are normally an essential element of all forms of popular design.

Strong primary colors work best with the cheaper printing techniques, and clear, bold, unfussy design makes an immediate attention-grabbing impact. The increased spending power of the young has encouraged a wide range of exciting youth-based designs.

Popular combinations of colors tend to concentrate on strong contrasts rather than on subtle harmonies, and the active colors — such as yellow, red, and orange, often combined with black — give an impression of energy.

POPULAR

Color Associations

The exclusive is usually related to styles or products reserved for the few, set aside for a particular individual or group, more often than not a privileged minority. Such products include top-of-the-line automobiles, designer fashions, leather accessories, perfumes, antiques, limited edition furnishings, and advertising for expensive restaurants.

Darkness suggests richness and restraint, so exclusivity is sometimes suggested by the deep wine reds, navy blues, olive greens, and deep chocolate browns, contrasted with buffs and creams.

Black and crimson are traditionally associated with formality, authority, and dignity, and silver is symbolic of coolness, restraint, and expense. In the ancient world, the most highly prized color was Tyrian purple, the production of which was so laborious and expensive that the color was reserved exclusively for the imperial rulers.

Right: Black is normally associated with sophistication and gold with luxury. In this advertisement shot for Gianna's Art Deco soap these associations have been combined to create a package design which encapsulates the concept of the product – in this case a top-of-the-line luxury item. This aspect is emphasized by the use of black and gold for the marble and for the dancing figures. The reworking of period design such as Art Deco is often associated with luxury goods because it tends to suggest an exclusive atmosphere.

Above: One of the main features of any exclusive design is that it can afford to be low-key, since the emphasis is on quality rather than quantity. In this advertisement for Paul Masson Californian wine, the designer has drawn on the classic labelling style used by the best French vineyards to convey the feeling that this is a quality wine. Even the special offer information is discreet and unobtrusive, whereas in everyday products such as detergent or breakfast cereals it it usually designed as a bright red flash across the package.

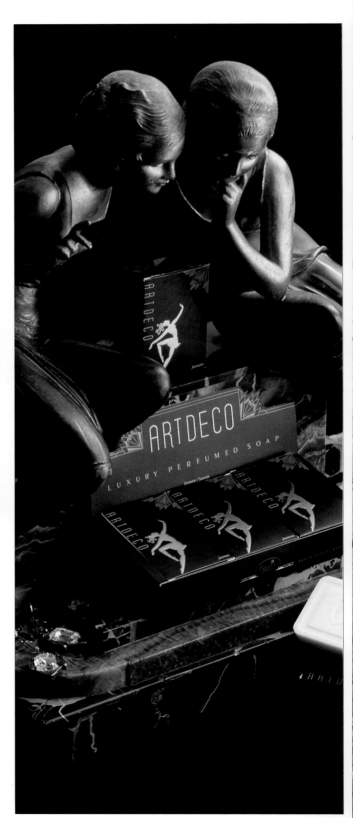

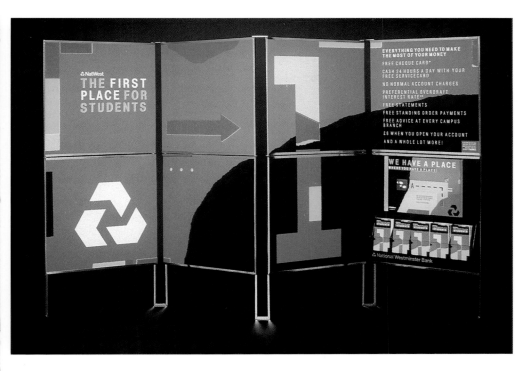

Popular color use tends to be the expected choice, which relies on brightness rather than subtlety for its impact. Common associations of the popular are with items and images intended to appeal to a wide variety of tastes – usually at the inexpensive end of the market – with youth, and with entertainment. Reds, oranges, yellows, and purples – the bright colors of the fairground – also translate well into the cheaper materials that are now used in many mass-market products.

Bright colors with easy-to-read simple graphics, and cheaply produced synthetics, such as plastic and nylon, changed both the design and manufacture of many goods in the 1950s. Plastic bottles in bright colors replaced traditional glass, and new printing techniques brought four-color printing into almost every form of packaging. Images from mass-market entertainment – the movies and comics in particular – were recreated in advertising, and the new music of the modern youth culture, the fast-food restaurants, and a burgeoning candy and soft drinks market responded to the growing number of popular market consumers, with more money to spend on non-essential goods than in previous decades.

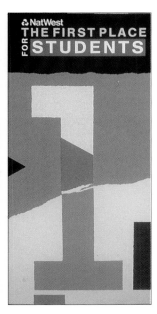

Left and above: In this bulletin board promoting Britain's National Westminster Bank's service for high school and college students, and in their promotional literature, the designers have managed to create a youthful, but at the same time thoughtful, image. Blue is generally regarded as promoting contemplation and reflection (right for a design aimed at promoting students to think about their finances) but the use of other bright primary colors, split into irregular flashes of color, helps to create a lively and energetic atmosphere. The lettering changes from white to yellow for maximum legibility against the background, because it needs to be read from a distance. The highly saturated blue background is eye-catching without being too aggressive.

Right: This lemon tea package for the Brooke Bond PG range makes use of a very obvious color association, the bright citrus yellow of the package reflecting the lemon element of the tea. The keynotes of much popular design are vivid colors, simple, easy-to-read graphics, and a clear message. This package obeys all the rules, and also has the advantage of good "standout" on the shelf, yellow being one of the most visible colors in the spectrum.

Combinations of Hue

Though exclusiveness might be epitomized by the promotion of perfumes, cosmetics, and designer fashion, it can be extended to include a wide range of top-of-the-line products from books to furnishings.

The combinations of colors for these products are often restrained, and the palette restricted to two or three. Silver and cream are often combined with dark, rich "Renaissance" colors of wine red, deep greens, and dark blues, for example.

Black has always had connotations of exclusivity and sophistication, particularly when allied with exclusive materials, such as exotic, foreign Black Sobranie cigarettes, often combined with gold lettering.

Even bright primaries and fluorescent colors can gain an exclusive feel when contrasted with black rather than white.

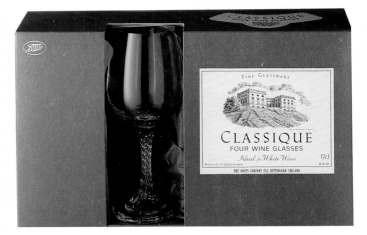

Left and below: In this line of glassware for Boots, the British drugstore chain, the package design has attempted to clarify the purpose of the different styles of glasses, using whiskey- or wine-style labels, as appropriate for each range. The colors are muted and elegant, with complementary hues used for the tissue paper packaging, another "quality range" component. The grays, greens, crimson and mauves create a toning but identifiably different element for each package. The labels are individual, but follow the theme of "classic" wine and whiskey labelling with traditional typography on a white background.

Left: In this coordinated package, bottle, and label design for a quality beer, subtle combinations of green, gold, rust, and mauve have strong "natural" associations, the beer being promoted as a wholesome, pure, and natural product. Outlining the brand-name "Erlanger" with a black line and shadowing has helped it stand out, while allowing it to remain an integral part of the overall design.

Monochromatic combinations and rich Renaissance colors, often combined with black, indicate exclusivity. Exclusive combinations imply: Rarity, richness, individuality.

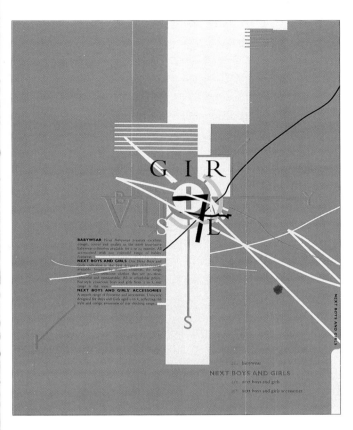

Popular color combinations are typically brash, brassy, and eye-catching. All the most readily identifiable hues of the color circle – red, yellow, green, and blue, separated and enhanced by black contours – can be used in any number of combinations to give a general impression of energy, humor, and light-heartedness, evoking the brilliantly mixed colors of a candy store or an amusement park.

Popular taste changes constantly and can be expected to follow seasonal and social trends, in which there is usually an appetite for the new. In general, young children show preferences for vivid reds and yellows, whereas more mature tastes swing toward the more mature crimsons, deeper blues and neutrals.

Promoting goods using a combination of bright colors and typography can give the designer problems of legibility, but tonal differences can be used to help the type to be legible. Care is needed, however, to ensure that the combinations do not cancel one another out by competing for attention.

Left: An own-brand pack of party glasses for Bloomingdale's department store provides another example of popular design with a sophisticated edge. Here contrasting colors – orange, green and mauve – have been used but blend together by virtue of all being low in saturation. The reversed typography of the words "Party Set" form part of the design.

COLOR VARIATIONS

Printer' process colors and vivid, highly saturated primaries, in sharp contrasts, have a popular, modern feel. Popular combinations imply: Vigour, enthusiasm, vitality.

Above: In this section opener from the Next Directory, a recently-launched mail-order catalog, the bright colors (blue and orange) often associated with popular products have been cleverly combined to create a very modern idiom, entirely in keeping with a company whose main aim is good design at budget prices. The split type, small print, and asymmetric arrangement is typical of the way in which modern design has advanced from the less sophisticated images and typography of the 1950s and 1960s.

Right: Shopping bags for a Japanese department store make use of black contrasted with flashes of bright primary colors. The simple "K" logo stands out from the background in both the red-based and black-based colorways, as does the white lettering for the name of the store, "Kintetsu". Another example of popular but sophisticated design, with the emphasis on strong graphic form so typical of Japanese design.

Tone and Saturation

Selections of colors that correspond most closely to a feeling for the exclusive are the darker shades of red, green, and blue, together with burnt, earthy browns and neutral gray, black, white, and cream. Combinations of high-key pastel and primary colors are out of place unless used very sparingly and subordinated to large background expanses of deep-toned colors, or black. Darker and lighter tones, and paler saturations of a single hue, can create an impression of confident restraint and elegance.

In general, exclusive color combinations are dominated by dark-toned muted colors, suggestive of dignity, gravity, and authority. The exclusive design should project an image of calm self-assurance, as though nothing in the design needed changing or improving. By definition, sophistication implies careful preparation, unhurried judgment, and attention to detail, culminating in a harmonious whole based on thought, refinement, and discrimination.

Below: This packaging for high-quality brandy obeys the basic principles of using rich deep colors with touches of gold, to convey an impression of exclusivity, luxury, and quality. The most expensive of the three, the 25-year-old brandy, is appropriately in the richest-looking combination.

Left: In this combined jar and container design for a superior brand of fruit syrup, the botanical drawings, limited color palette, and cool blue and green combination gives an impression of traditional values, of reliability and purity. The cloth cover with the string and seal has similar connotations.

COLOR VARIATIONS

Dark tone

Mid tone

Light tone

Full saturation

Mid saturation

Low saturation

Top: The darker tones usually have a more exclusive feel than the paler ones.

Above: Higher saturations are mostly combined with darker tones to create a more exclusive impression.

The overall assessment of tone is determined by a number of visual factors. These include the relationship of lighter or darker colors on the printed surface, how matte or glossy the material is that carries the design, and the intensity and color balance of the light sources used to illuminate goods in the display or retail setting. Strong contrasts of tone are ideal for providing good visibility and legibility. Combined with shiny materials, such as cellophane or metallic finishes, bright highlights from light sources can further enhance the glittering or glistening attractiveness of a popular product or design.

Combinations of highly saturated colors promote a showy popularity and add emotional excitement to any design or display. In other respects, color combinations are most dazzling when the tonal values of adjacent colors are close together, such as a combination of magenta and green, or a deep yellow with a very pale blue or violet.

To make the message less dazzling, it pays to dull the saturation of some of the colors.

Above: A variety of teas, featuring different blends in different packs, under the single brand name of Ashby's, has achieved an integrated look by using diverse combinations of colors, all within a range of tone and saturation giving the packs a shared identity. The combination of colorways and the different design on each teapot provided a clue to the blend of tea inside. The type is legible, but not dramatic, and the colors have been well chosen to stand out against the backgrounds.

Right: In these packs of a supermarket's own-brand chips, differences in tone and saturation have been used to create the graphic shapes, with the most highly saturated colors forming the background of each design.

COLOR VARIATIONS

Dark tone

Mid tone

Light tone

Full saturation

Mid saturation

Low saturation

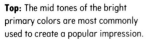

Top: The mid tones of the bright primary colors are most commonly used to create a popular impression.

Above: The highest saturations are needed to produce the standout associated with popular colors.

Shapes and Edges

The shapes most commonly associated with sophistication and dignity are often the simplest, and yet most perfect, of geometrical forms, such as the circle, the square, or the triangle, although the diamond and ellipse can also look elegant.

What is regarded as exclusive may change from decade to decade, as tastes and fashions alter, but the forms are those which appeal to the sophisticated palette of the time. When popular taste opts for hardedged functionalism, exclusive forms will probably be elaborate, highly wrought and decorative, or vice versa. Today, in an age of

mass-production which concentrates on simplified shapes suitable for machines, the exclusive tends to concentrate on elaborate, hand-crafted forms.

Right: The unusual shape of the bottle immediately conveys an impression of individuality and distinction as does the engraving of the medallion on the bottle, repeated in print on the box label, the simple dignity of the plain but elegant box.

Below: In this poster for the French newsmagazine L'Express, an almost monochromatic design, with a few touches of red, instantly creates a sophisticated image. The simple black line draws attention to the strong graphic form of the design.

14910 Ventura Blvd., Sherman Oaks, California 91403 213-990-8683

COLOR VARIATIONS

The forms – the shapes and edges – that confine different colors affect our perception of them. The exclusive is suggested by:
- singularity of form
- precision of edge
- passive forms

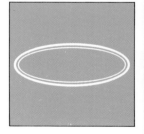

Popular imagery tends to remain what it has always been – an appeal to the most obvious instincts – loud and animated. Simple shapes in flat, vivid colors, separated by bold black outlines, were originally popular to mask the poor alignment of cheap printing. The brash appeal of the busy active forms and bright colors of the comic or seaside postcard lives on in many forms of popular product design.

Strident contrasts of primary colors in broad, flat shapes, often separated by bold black outlines, are quickly visible and get the message across simply at a very direct level.

Large, fat typefaces in strong colors, outlined in black to stand out over equally strong background colors, serve to emphasize a design with a strong, uncomplicated nature.

Above: A set of vibrant packages designed to appeal to popular tastes has been used to market Leopardi's ice cream. Combinations of 15 different candy colours were deliberately chosen to package the individual flavors, the color contrasts and highly decorative scrolled design creating an exotic "fun" atmosphere aimed at the perceived youthful market for the product.

Right: This jacket for a recent book on how to draw comics has drawn on the design style of the comics of the 1950s and 1960s. Broken images and a range of type styles, along with the figure typically leaping out of its surround, all help to create an impression of liveliness, energy, and power. The contrast of red and blue is a deliberate eye-catching device, the legibility of the lettering improved by outlining in black.

COLOR VARIATIONS

The forms – the shapes and edges – that confine different colors affect our perception of them. The popular is suggested by:
- variety of form
- quickly drawn lines
- active shapes and edges
- outlined shapes

Size and Proportion

Exclusiveness is generally associated with designs which are unemphatic and restrained and in which all the elements or components of the design are brought together to create an exquisitely balanced whole. An overall feeling of grandeur is combined with a fastidious (although strictly hidden) attention to detail, often by offsetting large, open expanses of color with small, thoughtfully placed images or areas of type.

Exclusive designs usually succeed in promoting a feeling of spaciousness and economy in which a few carefully selected colors, simple, elegant shapes, and refined textures are balanced together with poise and perfection. The immediate impression is one of harmony and cohesion. While exclusive design is influenced by the changing tastes of fashion – and to be chic or exclusive is often to be in the height of fashion – it also appears to incorporate qualities of permanence and perfection which transcend passing styles and popular trends.

Left: The subtle mixtures of colors, and gold, and the asymmetric and abstract design help to express the company's design attitudes – modern, tasteful, restrained, and exclusive.

Above: The simplified classic design, combined with the use of color are a clear indication that the product needs no further embellishment – the name alone sells the contents.

COLOR VARIATIONS

How a color is perceived is determined by the colors that surround it, and partly by the size and proportion of the colors relative to each other. Differing proportions have been used here to show some of the effects that can be achieved as a result.

Any product that has to appeal to a large sector of the market, thereby earning the adjective "popular", has also to appeal to a wide range of tastes, most of which are relatively unsophisticated. Bold typography, simple graphics, and strong colors often get the message across most easily and most strongly.

A large and important sector of the popular market is associated with the production and promotion of children's toys and clothes. Once the children are old enough to choose for themselves, they are often impressed by size and attracted by bright colors.

Size has a similar emphasis in the adult popular market, here equated with value for money. It is no accident, for example, that boxes of breakfast cereal are large in scale, to give the customer this impression, besides appealing to the natural instinct to feed the family and start off the day well.

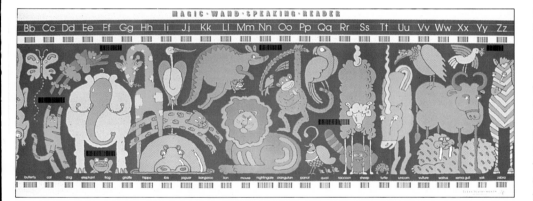

POPULAR

COLOR VARIATIONS

How a color is perceived is determined by the colors that surround it, and partly by the size and proportion of the colors relative to each other. Differing proportions have been used here to show some of the effects that can be achieved as a result.

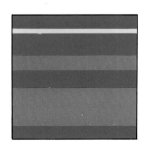

Top: Designing promotional literature for concepts like banking, health, or insurance is more liberating, but more difficult, than designing images for an instantly recognizable product like coffee or ice cream. In this brochure for Britain's National Westminster Bank, the designers have used arresting images, mainly by surprising the beholder with curious crops and proportions, to illustrate a series of proverbs about sound money sense. The fragmenting of the images gives the design a lively, and youthful appearance, and the choice of colors is aimed at a student market rather than the normal middle-aged, possibly conservative, customer.

Above left: In this alphabet wall-frieze, clever use has been made of stylized shapes and a limited palette of repeating colors to give a pattern and unity to the concept – a different animal for each letter of the alphabet. The curly shapes and blended colors make it suitable for very young children, removing any aggressive or frightening element from the design.

Pattern and Texture

An exclusive impression is exhibited by designs in which a few carefully selected elements are regularly repeated to create a unified pattern that combines simplicity with spaciousness and order. A taste for the exclusive can vary from the richly patterned and decorated to the plain and unadorned. Where pattern is included, it should function as an integral part of the design, rather than as something arbitrarily applied. In general, it should appear restrained, tasteful, and elegant.

"Truth to materials" is a good rule to follow in selecting textures, so that exclusive or upmarket designs in wood, glass, leather, fabric, or metal are ideally allowed to exhibit their appropriate surface qualities. On paper, card, or plastic, high-quality reproductions of natural textures, such as wood grain or tooled leather, will often help convey an upmarket image. For many centuries, fur was a powerful symbol of exclusiveness, its role now taken over by smooth leathers or richly textured tweeds, or the more intimately sensual sheen of satin, silk, and velvet.

Right: The subtle combination of greens, golds and browns is often used to indicate exclusivity, and the smallness of the lettering also implies that the product needs no advertisement.

Below: Although gold is not usually legible on a mid-green ground, the subtlety of the combination coupled with the very glossy finish of the whole bag give a quality feel to the product.

Exclusive patterns tend to be restrained, elegant, and dignified, and are often combined with natural textures such as wood or silk.

Above: This promotional material for the city of Glasgow has made good use of popular images of the city, with a range of typography styles and image sizes and patterns, to create a lively, friendly look for a city not previously renowned for its accessibility.

It is usually color, rather than shape or pattern, that appeals first to less sophisticated tastes, although patterned surfaces are usually more popular than plain ones.

To be truly popular, patterns and textures have to appeal to a wide range of interests and age groups. Photography, collage and photo-montage have become particularly popular in contemporary design, partly because of the easy availability of source material, and the speed with which it can be assembled, but also because the drawing skills of graphic designers have been overtaken by the manipulative skills of the computer-aided designer, with immediate access to an astonishing number of patterns and textures at the touch of a button.

Trends in the approach to pattern and texture permeate slowly through to the popular end of the market. A pattern associated with an expensive product may well be copied in a cheaper one, after the former has proved its worth, possibly with minor changes of color and design. Equally a product geared for the exclusive market in an expensive natural fabric may be copied in cheaper synthetics for mass production.

COLOR VARIATIONS

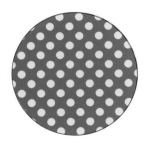

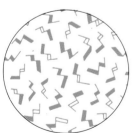

Popular patterns take many forms but are usually executed in bright colors and form an obvious part of the overall design.

Below: These brilliantly patterned packs of fireworks say it all. The sparkling, fizzing, overall design in brilliant colors leaves the beholder in no doubt as to the exciting nature of the contents, and makes the pack an almost irresistible purchase. The traditional typography and the Victorian style of the branding – Brock's Amazing Fireworks – emphasize the traditional nature of firework displays, and help give the impression that the brand name is a long-established leader in the field, with its implication of reliability and performance.

INDIVIDUAL

Nothing designed by a committee is likely to be original or in any way out of the ordinary. The individual, however, is answerable to no one, with a resulting freedom of expression that makes a fertile breeding ground for new, offbeat, and different concepts.

Colors that have the power to surprise and arrest attention – particularly in odd or unusual combinations – include the highly saturated reds, yellows, and oranges, particularly when combined with pinks, purples, and acid greens.

Conventional wisdom is usually turned on its head in an individual approach, and computer-aided design, with its ability to combine illustration and type in free, informal mixes gives today's designer a whole new range of options.

separate

singular

nonconformist

egocentric

distinctive

personalized

independent

segregated

personal

joint

collective

agreeable

altruistic

shared

amalgamated

interdependent

united

communal

The corporate approach is, by definition, the agreed line and the safe and tested response to a situation or product. The colors chosen are likely to be the traditionl ones – such as the dark blues, greens, and browns of school colors – which make equally good choices for corporate images for much the same reasons.

The combinations of colors will err on the safe side, helping to enhance the impression of corporate solidarity and financial security. Gold and silver lettering on a rich dark red or blue background helps to give the impression of solid worth and long-established values.

The novel, the untried and untested, rarely has a place in the corporate approach, and typography is likely to be cautious rather than adventurous. Pattern and texture are most likely to be geometric and repetitive, adding to the feeling of reassurance and reliability.

CORPORATE

Color Associations

Individuality of color is enhanced when an easily namable color – red, yellow, green, or blue – is presented in isolation against a neutral ground of white, gray, black, or silver. This approach works well when a particular color has already established itself firmly in the mind of the customer in relation to a specific product. The distinctive red can of Coca Cola and the yellow pack of Kodak photographic film are internationally recognized examples.

To rank as individual, the design has to differentiate itself from others in its category. In terms of color, this can be done by "shocking" the viewer – a familiar object can be colored in a different way or unexpected colors can be used. Although in color personality tests, it is the choice of purples, reds, and yellows that most indicate an individual's desire to stand out from the crowd, in design terms this simply means using color in novel or unusual ways.

86 **ORIGINALS**
Originals Originals presents a complete wardrobe; from contemporary formal classics through to relaxed casualwear. All Next Directory original classics are found here.

103 **EVENINGWEAR**
White Hot Essentially a white hot, tone on tone story, moving from relaxed easy-to-wear through to classic occasional dress. Masquerade A black and brights story inspired by harlequins and masquerades.

Left: An intense, personalized palette of strong hues enhances the bold motifs of this design. The image is overwhelming, the typographic information secondary. The powerful color treatment and interesting edge qualities of the motifs demand the viewer's attention, aiming to stimulate curiosity about the message of the poster.

Above: A bright color used in a very dominant way can be risky in design terms; the stronger the color, the stronger the response. Individuality is indicated in dynamic use of pure, clear hues to make a positive statement. This section-opener from a clothes catalog is unconventional in its context, using bold abstract imagery and vivid color.

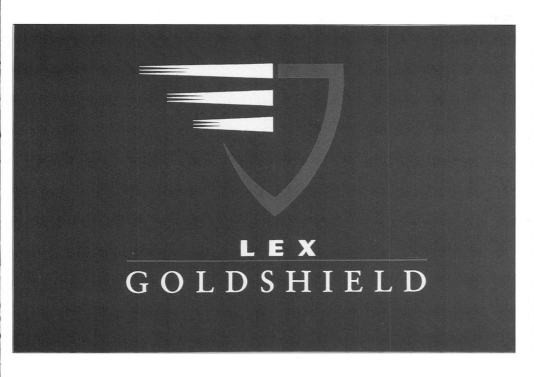

LEX

GOLDSHIELD

Most well-established companies or corporations have a vested interest in putting themselves over to the public as solid, dependable, and strong. The most reassuring choices for letterheads or sales literature are the honest blues and earthy browns, combined with white to symbolize virtue. Bright, frivolous colors are usually inappropriate because they undermine confidence in the seriousness of the organization. Exceptions include the relatively recent use of primary colors in the brochures and graphics of banks, insurance and investment companies, who are deliberately trying to widen their appeal to include the youthful segment of the market.

Above: This relatively bright blue is an extremely dense color and therefore establishes a solid presence appropriate to a corporate image. The light golden brown of the shield shape stands for gold, associating the visual elements with the company name. The white flashes suggest an active, forward-moving quality and make a formal link with the clearly legible white type.

Right: Compare the overall impression of this design solution with the character conveyed by the one above. The same basic color elements have been chosen to suggest reliability and strength, but they are more muted in tone. Likewise the type and logo are very discreet, representing the more restrained approach commonly applied to corporate work.

Combinations of Hue

The most conspicuous and optically expansive of all colors is yellow. When surrounded by a contrasting color it appears to radiate beyond its physical boundary and spread itself into the neighboring color area. Yellow is least conspicuous when set against a light-toned background – white or cream, for example – and at its most assertive when contrasted with black, dark blue, or violet. The yellow then appears to advance, just as lighter and warmer reds and oranges advance and detach themselves from darker and cooler greens and blues.

One way in which a design can achieve individuality is by using unexpected "clashing" combinations of colors – shocking pink and red, for example, or yellow and purple. The effect of the clashes can be heightened by the proportions of the colors used, and by the use of typography, maybe using a "negative" image, where the type is reversed out of the darker ground.

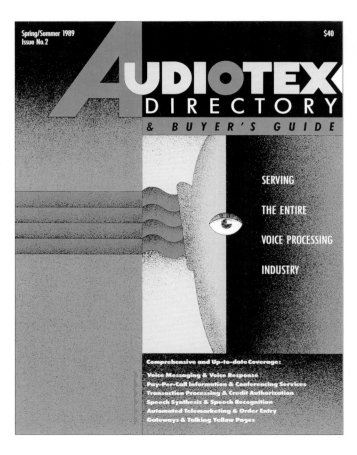

Above: The primary color combination of red, yellow, and blue often appears brash, but the way it is applied to the image and texture of this magazine page utilizes the lively character of these strong hues without seeming garish. This is due to the complex textural qualities of the design, deriving from the detail of the photographic image and the impact of the colored type.

Left: This is an unusual and effective color combination – none of the hues or tones seems an obvious choice, but they work extremely well together. They are all relatively high-key compared with the expected color character – green is more often used as a mid-tone than a pale pastel, for example. To anchor the white type and give it maximum clarity, black toning is applied to the type areas.

COLOR VARIATIONS

Eccentric combinations and strong contrasts give a feeling of individuality. Individual combinations imply: Quirkiness, novelty, change.

Corporations are dependent on team work to maintain the stability and growth of their operations. Typical colors intended to project an appropriately positive image to the potential investor or recruit include harmonious combinations of black, white, gold and silver typography with substantial medium-to-deep blues, browns and greens, such as cobalt, cornflower and royal blues, Delft blue and Prussian blue, ultramarine and navy blue, leather and tobacco brown, teak, chestnut and mahogany, umber and sienna earths, and jade and deep bottle and olive greens.

Financial institutions favor deep-blue associations of order, conservatism and reliability. Deep greens, suggesting abundance and reassurance, are popular with established department stores. Where brighter colors are used, they are often added in limited areas for small touches of definition: a bright red or emerald green rule, for example, or a brightly colored fine rule box around a design.

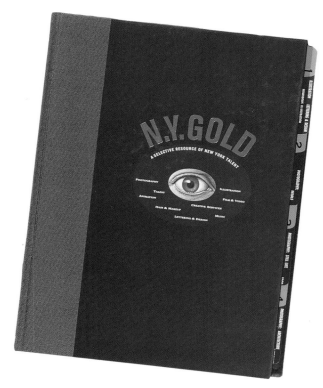

COLOR VARIATIONS

Dark, rich colors in sober combinations create a corporate image. Corporate combinations imply: Reassurance, solidarity, resolve.

Above: Black provides an air of sophistication suited to upscale styling, and this impression is enhanced by the use of blue foil blocking for the title, so that light as well as color becomes an element of the design. Tiny touches of red and green provide decorative contrast. The cover displays a direct and confident approach to color typography likely to make an impact on the design-conscious level of the corporate world at which the sourcebook is aimed.

Above: This again represents the classic corporate color scheme, with the added embellishment of gold foil blocking. Broad quarter-binding on the spine in warm brown balances the dominant area of blue. The central eye motif is described naturalistically in lighter tones of the main colors, so this is a harmonious element. The bright yellow page tags are an enlivening detail designed to be conscpicuous and accessible.

Tone and Saturation

The importance of promoting individuality in connection with marketing and selling a particular item is largely a result of the market being flooded with a range of products that look, taste, and perform in identical ways. The promotion of the product then depends on how well its individuality can be remembered by the purchaser.

Since color vision is normally most sensitive to yellow – it has unmatched lightness of tone with fullness of saturation – a combination of yellow and black is particularly eye-catching. It is important for a designer to be aware of competing products and competing color schemes, but any design for, say, supermarket shelves must be capable of being read at a distance. Lower saturations will fail to stand out against stronger ones, and darker tones will recede against lighter ones.

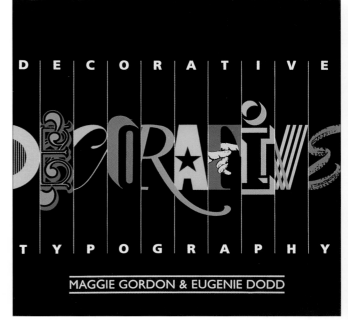

Above: This commissioned illustration works with a limited but inventive color range. The light-tone beige areas stand out but the bright yellow logo, though small, is competitive because both light in tone and highly saturated. The blue and purple are fairly strong in saturation but tonally the blue is more visible, as shown by the monochrome version.

Above: This book cover demonstrates the individualistic approach in both the forms and colors of the type, illustrating a preference for snappy or unusual combinations. The colors are light to mid-tones that read very effectively against black and are intensified by it. The black background also successfully holds down potential color interactions – blue and green are recessive colors while pink and yellow typically advance – so that the decorative type remains legible as one word.

COLOR VARIATIONS

Dark tone

Mid tone

Light tone

Full saturation

Mid saturation

Low saturation

Top: The mid tones in the individual palette of colors can be combined to create a quirky feel.

Above: Medium to high saturations are likely to give the strongest sense of individuality.

deally the corporate identity should reassure rather than shock. Strong contrasts of tone and saturation are probably better avoided in favor of more subtle combinations, providing of course that legibility is retained where this is an important element of the design. Deep blue and cream may give a more solid-looking and more traditional appearance than deep blue and white, and dark red and pale gray than dark red and white.

Most of the highly saturated colors have a rather youthful appeal and are therefore not appropriate for company images reflecting maturity and experience. Where the corporate image is aimed at a younger section of the market, the more highly saturated colors and stronger contrasts will help put a positive image across.

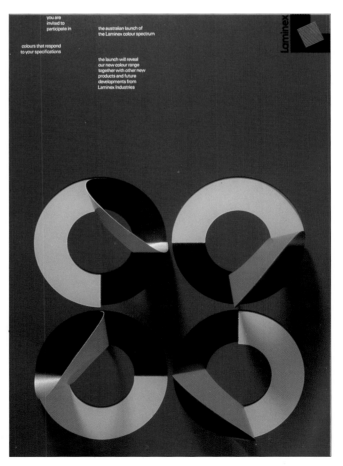

Above: Bright corporate colors may be used by public service companies for instant identification. This collage-style U.K. brochure cover is dominated by the Royal Mail's high-saturation red and yellow, contrasted with cold blue and lilac and with the tonal density of black. At left, a green-blue complement to the red throws forward the neutral gray applied to the "engraved" symbol.

Right: This promotional literature for a company specializing in color, launched a new product range with an image that succeeds in conveying both the solid worth of the company (the dark-blue ground and wide-based design) with innovative ideas — the use of contrasting and abstract shapes and warm-toned colors to give the design an unexpected lift.

COLOR VARIATIONS

Dark tone

Mid tone

Light tone

Full saturation

Mid saturation

Low saturation

Top: The mid to dark tones of the corporate range of colors produce the most stable and harmonious effect.

Above: The mid saturations, combined with darker tones, create a feeling of strength and security.

Shapes and Edges

In promoting the individual, the designer is often concerned with inventing or sustaining the real or imaginary character of a product or brand-name. Not only color but also shape can help the customer to recognize quickly his or her favorite choices on shelves lined with similar goods. Coca-Cola, for example, is traditionally recognized as much by the distinctive shape of its bottle, as by the colors and typography of its branding.

When searching the cabinet for a particular drink, the shape of the bottle is often the most identifiable factor. Shape and edge can therefore be of considerable help in picking out the individual in a group. Star shapes can be used successfully for "money off" labels on products, and decorative borders, shadowed lettering, scrolls, and flags can all be used to add individuality to a design.

Above: The simple white shapes serve to emphasize the idiosyncratic message of this poster.

Above right: This busy, personalized design is cleverly crafted to combine the many varied elements successfully. The patterns and motifs introduce a wide range of shapes and edge qualities, but these are held together by color links traveling throughout the surface. For clarity, the white type is laid on areas of solid color.

COLOR VARIATIONS

The forms – the shapes and edges – that confine different colors affect our perception of them. The individual is suggested by:
- unusual forms
- asymmetric shapes
- hand-drawn lettering or uneven letter spacing
- contrasts of form

INDIVIDUAL

Above: The classic brown and blue corporate combination gains an extra touch of sophistication from the bronzed metallic sheen. The high contrast of black and white gives crisp definition to the hard-edged shapes. The checkered bands and sideline type draw attention to the real edges of the objects. It is unusual to push the information to the edge of the design, but this gives prominence to the logo.

BRITAIN
AT
EXPO '92

Above: The shapes and colors of the British flag are used here as a promotional device for Expo 92. The color combination of red, white, and blue refers, in effect, to the corporate identity of the nation. This geometric arrangement re-orders the actual divisions of the flag into a fractured, energetic image, both in abstract terms and in the figurative sense that the angular lines form the shape of a walking man. The formal arrangement of the design is carried through in the clean shapes of the slanted sanserif type.

Companies wishing to emphasize the old-established traditions, whether genuine or not, like to adopt the shapes and devices of heraldry, such as shields and crests.

It is also quite common to find companies or professional organizations of recent origin favoring the use in their logos of simple geometric shapes, such as regular polygons, suggesting the amalgamation of separate units into an integrated whole. Regular grids are popular for much the same reason.

The most successful company logos are those which are easily memorable and seem at a glance to sum up the essence, character, or function of the organization they seek to represent.

Financial or manufacturing corporations, eager to emphasize the efficiency and reliability of their operations, generally prefer the spacious orderliness and impersonality of crisp, sanserif typefaces, such as Univers and Helvetica. The overall desire is to promote a durable image of individual parts contributing to a unified whole, as occurs with the five interlocking rings (representing the five continents) adopted to symbolize the modern Olympic Games.

COLOR VARIATIONS

The forms – the shapes and edges – that confine different colors affect our perception of them. The corporate is suggested by:
- evenly spaced lettering
- balanced shapes
- horizontally biased design
- squares, rectangles and circles

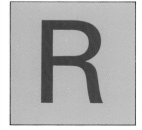

Size and Proportion

In a textile design it is generally acceptable to use repeating patterns in which each component or motif contributes equally to the overall effect. In graphic design, intended usually to convey information in a specific order, or emphasize one visual component more than another, it is generally inadvisable to have several colors or design elements competing for equal amounts of attention. Instead, it is better to organize a visual hierarchy in which some parts of the design are permitted to demand attention more than others. When seeking to stress individuality, the effect can be exaggerated, so that one design feature is permitted to dominate all others, as with a banner headline on the front page of a newspaper. If such a feature is colored or shaped in an individual way, it does not need to be especially large.

Individual implies unconventional, and this interpretation can be suggested by designs in which the components appear imbalanced, eccentric, or distinctly oddly proportioned.

Above: These color areas are divided about equally and whereas a solid dark blue would be too heavy, the half-tone retains the balance. The colors are individually printed, not derived from the four-color process.

Above: The expanse of green obviously dominates this design, but it is cleverly balanced by the curving cradle of the white shape and by the intensity of the red dot. The color contrast would give visibility even if the red area was small type.

COLOR VARIATIONS

How a color is perceived is determined by the colors that surround it, and partly by the size and proportion of the colors relative to each other. Differing proportions have been used here to show some of the effects that can be achieved as a result.

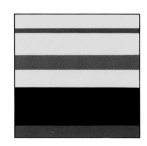

Above: A design alluding to the colors of the French flag incorporates classic symbols of French design within the color bands. The white space is a positive element that offsets the density of the blue and red. The type area is small in relation to the image, but perfectly legible.

The positive aspect of the corporate aim is to reinforce an image in which the resources of the company are pooled to achieve a combined effect which is greater than the sum of the individual parts.

The designer may have to promote the concept that all the contributors are equals as part of the whole and, by definition, the corporate body consists of a group of contributors who forfeit their individuality to the greater good of this whole.

Corporate literature is produced to reflect various aspects of a company's business, so size and proportion are important. The design should be uncluttered and well paced, with careful attention given to the proportions of picture to text and white space. Configurations of regular proportions combined with colors of roughly equal visual impact might be used. Whatever the emphasis, the overall effect is ideally one in which all the elements blend together to create a single, unified design.

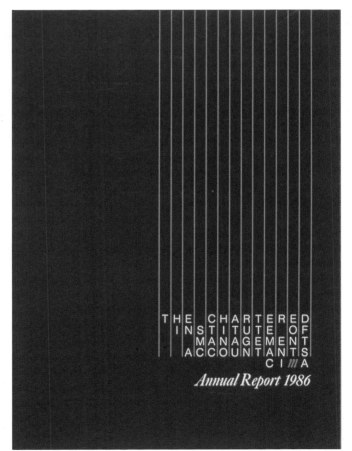

Above: This very solid blue, implying strength and reliability, is enlivened by the vertical band of fine pink stripes, carefully calculated in width and overall proportion to the format achieving impact without appearing "loud." Horizontal stress in the confined area of white type completes the balance of the design.

COLOR VARIATIONS

How a color is perceived is determined by the colors that surround it, and partly by the size and proportion of the colors relative to each other. Differing proportions have been used here to show some of the effects that can be achieved as a result.

Pattern and Texture

A design can afford to be individual or unconventional when produced for a special occasion, or when expense is not a limiting factor.

As a rule, a richly textured surface has more character and individuality than a plain one, although a simple pattern is often more memorable than a complex one. A design which combines contrasting elements of pattern and texture has a stronger individual appeal. Using unexpected materials can create an impression of individuality, as can hand-drawn and hand-painted images or lettering.

Left: The pattern element in this design is eccentric and personalized, relating to the earth and sky in a range of motifs suited to the promotion of natural cosmetics. The exotic combination of viridian, black, and gold gives an intriguing Gothic character. In a typical solution to ensure that the product identity stands out, the logo is printed in white on the dark backgrounds.

VIVARIUM TIERPARK DÄHLHÖLZLI
NEUERÖFFNUNG 17. SEPTEMBER 1988

Left: The engraved texture of a naturalistic foliage design contrasts with the shoal of stylized fish that corresponds to the texture of the parrot's neck feathers. Touches of yellow emphasize the repetitive patterning quality of the fish. Overall, the colors relate to nature but are in themselves strong, artificial hues creating direct impact. Their graduated tones are offset by pale highlights, but there are no solid darks, so the general impression is high-key.

COLOR VARIATIONS

Individual patterns are often quirky and offbeat, possibly with several patterns used within one design, in an asymmetrical arrangement.

Right: Panels of regular pattern based on heraldic devices represent different aspects of a railfreight company's services. Strong hues and tonal contrasts are designed to make the company's image visible and recognizable at a distance and on the move, as seen in application on the freight train shown above.

If the overall image that a group, institution, or company wishes to portray is that of efficiency, authority, and reliability, the patterns are best confined to simple repeating ones, such as the vertical pin-stripes reminiscent of an executive's suit. Regular, geometrical grids reinforce a feeling of efficiency. Irregular or quirky patterns may be endearing but are probably out of place, unless intended to appeal to the young or off-beat, as might be the case perhaps when encouraging an unusually wide variety of individuals to join a club or enter an educational institution.

Newly introduced patterns, such as those exploiting recent developments in computer design, can be used to indicate that a company is on the ball and up-to-date with modern developments. Alternatively, continuity can be emphasized by reviving the decorative patterns and textures of a bygone age. It may be possible to reinforce an image of reliability and experience by adopting or revamping styles of typography and ornamentation from Victorian design, notably those of the Arts and Crafts movement, itself inspired by corporate workshop practices.

COLOR VARIATIONS

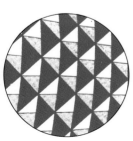

Corporate patterns may be even, stable, and repetitive, and ideally pattern and texture should blend into a unified whole.

Above: An atmospherically textured background makes an effective dark-toned field for the clean, simple shapes of the company logo and name. The colors of the symbol and type are relatively restrained, but easily read.

Gold lettering, especially a classic serifed type, has traditional associations implying a long-established business. It also provides an interesting surface quality because of the play of light.

TRADITIONAL

The term "traditional" tends to refer to anything that is long practiced, and applies as much to craft as it does to art. Concepts of what is traditional seem to be deeply rooted in some nostalgic rural past – in other words, they belong to the pre-Industrial Revolution period when almost all items were handmade.

The colors predominantly associated with traditional values and concepts are those that provide a reassuring solidity, often with earthy associations – the deep rich reds, dark greens, navy blues, and chestnut browns. Lettering is usually in serif faces with rounded forms, harking back to the original hand-cut typography of old manuscripts.

mellow

inherited

familiar

old-fashioned

trustworthy

conventional

reassuring

well-worn

relaxing

young

invented

unfamiliar

up-to-date

questionable

precocious

apprehensive

brand-new

exciting

Today's version of modern is tomorrow's version of traditional, although concepts which last even longer tend to become classic.

The modern color concepts of the 1980s and 1990s are clear and sharp, with clean lines and often starkly simple graphic shapes to contain them. Computer-aided design has changed the framework of contemporary graphic design, and text and color are now integrated in arresting and novel ways.

MODERN

Color Associations

In seeking to promote the traditional we are usually attempting to project an image of reassurance, often with the aim of selling products that have been tried and tested over many years. The traditional is usually associated with the era before mass production, and so any goods that have a "handmade" quality tend to benefit from this treatment.

The nostalgia associated with past traditions tends to be centered on an image of rural life, and the colors linked with nature – the greens, browns, and ochers of the land – are connected in our minds with tradition. Equally the colors often chosen for uniforms, packaging, and delivery trucks – burgundy, navy blue, and bottle green give a strong traditional feel, particularly when combined with gold and bronze.

Above: Every detail of this retail store evokes a traditional mood. The warm colors of the interior's brass and wood fittings create a solid, well-established presence. The logo, in a strong but not gaudy red on a parchment-colored background, uses 19th-century typography and the needle and thread image to imply a relationship to hand-crafted goods of the past. The company stationery (right) maintains the traditional identity in color and style, down to the brown paper bag supplied for wrapping small purchases.

Left: The classic combination of gold and dark green guarantees a traditional feel. A touch of red in this packaging enlivens the design. The pairing of red and gold typically suggests a heraldic association, as does the shield that bears the product name, which here also acts as a masculine symbol.

TRADITIONAL

102

In the early years of this century, designers began to react to the florid and overly ornate decorations of the Victorian era. As a result, there was a general swing toward the austere and undecorated, summed up in the popular slogan "form follows function" and evident in an economy and efficiency in which color choices were functional rather than esthetic.

The Modernist approach is particularly well suited to promoting and packaging technological goods, such as radios, televisions, computers, and electrical products in general. The plastics used to package these items are well suited to clear, vivid colors with an emphasis on the psychological primary colors: red, yellow, green, and blue, combined with black, white or silver and confined within simple geometric divisions of the design as a whole. One of the other characteristics of this approach is to let the material speak for itself so the grays and silvers of steel, aluminum, and concrete, for example, sometimes become the background for flashes of brighter color on smaller items.

Left: Red, pink, and orange have been traditionally regarded as clashing colors not to be used together. Modern design tends to enjoy such vivid interactions and here the colors are highly saturated, deliberately artificial, and thrown forward in full strength by the pale-toned background. Jazzy shapes and a "handwritten" lettering style also contribute to the contemporary mood.

Right: This computer design makes full use of the brilliance of printing process colors – yellow, magenta, and cyan. Used in this way, the colors are scintillating, artificial, and wholly unrepresentational, though applied to recognizable features of a composite image. The unexpected juxtapositions of various fragments of the image within the whole also demonstrate a specifically modern approach to design, in which abstract and surreal influences are presumed to be familiar and acceptable to the viewer.

Combinations of Hue

The traditional, earth-based colors of greens, ochers, brick reds, and browns in fairly subtle contrasts – green with gold, brick red or brown and cream – produce the strongest associations with the past. The soft mixtures of vegetable-dyed wools in traditional tweeds and early tapestries can be used to recreate a feeling of reassurance and permanence.

Gold, copper, and bronze are particularly valuable for typography, evoking the rich patrons of the Renaissance and echoing the gold leaf of illuminated manuscripts. Applied to promotions and products with an exclusive or handmade character, they give a feeling of permanence and luxury.

Above: This packaging demonstrates a unified range in which the same design in gold is applied to black, green, and red grounds. All are successful in terms of the gold type and borders maintaining legibility against the background colors. The stark white of the product name and cup stands out clearly for immediate identification.

Left: A low-key combination of pastel colors is evocative of a gentler age. The colors are similar in tone and would not read so well without the linear factor that provides clear definition: the type is outlined and the illustration is also discreetly anchored by keylines.

COLOR VARIATIONS

Dark-toned, rich colors in natural shades give a feeling of tradition and permanence. Traditional combinations imply: Quality, strength, safety.

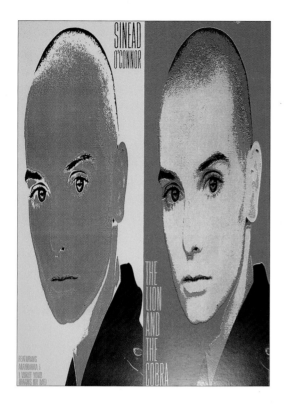

Left: Bright, rich colors used in a photographic context translate this dual image into a semi-abstract design. In the pink-magenta color range the face remains clearly readable. The more limited yellow/purple combination reduces the amount of recognizable detail, but the contemporary viewer has no difficulty in identifying the descriptive pattern of unrealistic color combinations.

The modern tends to be associated with clear and blatant combinations of all the colors in the color wheel. The introduction of new materials, and the ability to saturate plastics with vivid chemical dye-stuffs, previously unobtainable at economical prices, has allowed designers the opportunity to create arresting colors in products and in promotional material. The development of fluorescent and phosphorescent colors in the 1950s added to designers' palettes, and has allowed them to impart a vital, youthful, and exciting image to their work.

Preferred combinations of hue have altered over the decades. During the Bauhaus period, combinations of red, yellow, blue, black, and white were favored, with strong tonal differences in the designs, heavy black typography often being over-printed on red or yellow. Today clashes of brilliant orange, purple, pink, and yellow are favorite combinations for youth-oriented products.

COLOR VARIATIONS

Bright, highly saturated colors, in vivid contrasts or combined with black have a clear, modern feel. Modern combinations imply: Liveliness, wit, clarity.

Left: These colors are similar in character to those of the design above, but the range of hues is wider and they appear more brilliant against the black background. The typography is white on black, one of the strongest contrasts for legible type.

Tone and Saturation

Colors most typically associated with durability have a strong traditional feel. It has become almost a cliché when evoking a traditional image to give the colors the patina of age by reducing the saturation and darkening the tone to produce shades, rather like the faded colors of an ancient tapestry, or the muted hues of pressed flowers.

In packaging high-quality cookies, teas, herbs, jams, pickles, and relishes an appropriate feeling for the rural and the traditional is often promoted by using quiet contrasts of light-toned unsaturated colors. The typography often echoes this approach, and brown, burgundy, or navy blue inks are used instead of blacks to maintain the slightly faded charm associated with an English country house.

Left: This is a color combination that appears relatively even in tone and saturation, but the black and white version shows how the brown reads as a much darker tone and is used for definition. The intense, saturated red is a highlighting device that gives contrast against the mellow cream and brown coloring. Reversed white type lifts the lettering out from the detail of the design.

Above: A product of this kind needs careful management of the color elements, to create a harmonious relationship between package colors, typography, and imagery. The pastel colors chosen for the packs are naturally low key, and the marbled texture creates further restraint. The typography is designed to have greater contrast for legibility.

COLOR VARIATIONS

 Dark tone
 Mid tone
 Light tone

 Full saturation
 Mid saturation
 Low saturation

Top: The mid-tonal range is often used to produce a feeling of stability and tradition.

Above: Fairly full saturations, combined with mid tones, create a strong, but stable, impression that evokes the traditional atmosphere.

Fully saturated colors and lighter tones seem to embody the spirit of excitement and youth associated with modern design trends, partly as a deliberate rejection of the subtler shades and combinations of what is perceived to be traditional, although fashions change relatively quickly and today's idea of modern may be tomorrow's version of traditional or the retrospective.

Ever new forms of electric light have transformed the appearance of modern interiors, both domestic and commercial. Open-plan living, both in houses and offices, and greater use of glass, allowing in more natural light, have favored the use of brighter saturations of color which no longer overpower their surroundings, and are in keeping with modern architecture.

In street advertising the use of color discharge tubes provides a wide range of stimulating colors far higher in saturation than those of paints or inks, such as neon red, sodium vapor yellow, argon green, and mercury vapor blue.

The introduction of the laser provided light sources of even greater purity of color throughout the spectral range.

Above: Vivid, highly saturated colors create a sense of fun, but the variation of color combinations also injects a degree of sophistication. The type colors are carefully selected to read well against their background tones; for example, the subsidiary typography is white on the turquoise and red packs, but red on the yellow.

Above: Each of these strong, brilliant colors is highly distinctive, although as the black and white image shows, they are very close in tone. The design has an elegant simplicity in the use of a clean, unbusy arrangement of white typography on a solid, plain-color ground.

COLOR VARIATIONS

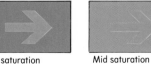

Dark tone | Mid tone | Light tone

Full saturation | Mid saturation | Low saturation

Top: Lighter saturations usually have a more up-to-date and modern feel than darker ones.

Above: Lighter saturations, combined with lighter tones, are often used to convey a modern image.

Shapes and Edges

The strident shapes and colors of medieval heraldry provide an inexhaustible supply of traditional images in the form of flags, banners, shields, plumes, ribbons, scrolls, and folds.

Since almost all ethnic groups possess a rich cultural heritage, their legacy can be used to provide forms that are appropriate for the message. Throughout the world, certain images are associated with particular cultures – the geometric mosaic shapes of Islam, the stylized flowers and birds of Japan, and so forth.

Repeating, stable patterns create a strong traditional feel, especially when organized in frames or borders. There are many sources for border patterns (including the designer's bible, *The Grammar of Ornament* by Owen Jones, 1856).

Serif faces that echo the brush strokes of calligraphy have a strong traditional feel, as does hand lettering and round-bodied type. Dropped capitals also give a traditional look.

Below: A symbolic image is given a sense of solidity by the use of muted colors with definite tonal contrast modeling the form. The dynamic shape of the symbol is allowed to stand free against an open background. A restrained approach to color is a typical feature of corporate design; bright colors do not suggest attributes such as security and continuity that well-established companies may want to convey.

Above: The shapes of shields, banners, and scrolls are all redolent of traditional values. In this design the color combination is totally sympathetic to the feel of the imagery; every element is in character.

NATIONAL MUTUAL LIFE

The forms – the shapes and edges – that confine different colors affect our perception of them. The traditional is suggested by:
- hand-drawn lettering
- solid, firm shapes with a strong base
- representational images

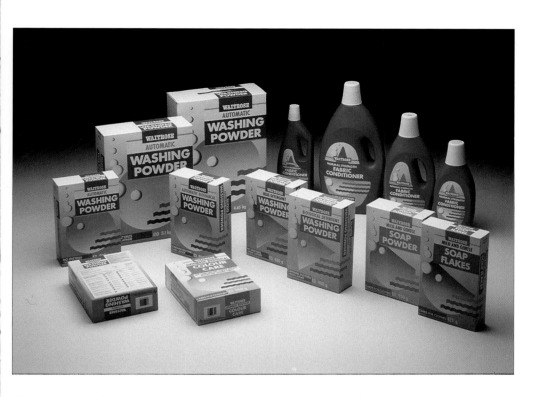

Much of modern design continues to reveal its debt to the abstract and formalist Constructivism of the early decades of this century. Simple and spacious forms are balanced to give a poised but often asymmetrical whole. Emphasis is on the horizontal, vertical, and diagonal, and on the simple and perfect forms of the square, the circle, and the equilateral triangle. Regularly geometrical grids also symbolize the mechanical efficiency of the modern.

Whereas traditional design often emphasizes a clear pictorial division between an advancing foreground and a receding background, modern design frequently presents us with an orientally inspired ambiguity of figure and ground. The modern designer must be as concerned with the shapes created by forms or typefaces as with the space that surrounds them.

The advent of computer-aided design has allowed much freer forms in the combination of type and color areas as far as printed material is concerned.

Above: These cleanly shaped, stylized symbols of water and bubbles have a formal character that is essentially modern. The weighty sansserif type stands out clearly on solid color, while the abstract imagery is defined in terms of tonal gradations matching light against dark to emphasize the shapes. The colors of the packs serve as identification, of both the product range and the company's own brand.

Below: Strong colors give weight to this design, to offset the intricacy of the cutout edges. The interplay of these bright colors with white is orchestrated to make the detail of the typography read easily while retaining the abstract character of the design.

COLOR VARIATIONS

The forms – the shapes and edges – that confine different colors affect our perception of them. The modern is suggested by:
- geometric or abstract shapes
- small lettering
- asymmetric design
- sanserif typography
- computer-generated forms

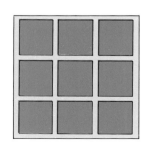

MON DÉSIR RESTAURANT

Size and Proportion

Traditional design gives the impression of reaching above and beyond the transitory nature of fads and fashions. Established conventions have stood the test of time, and suggest the shapes of goods made the way they always have been made, largely unaffected by passing trends because they need no improvement.

For almost all the foodstuffs, commodities, and tools we buy there is a conventional size and proportion associated with the package, much of it based on commonsense and known consumer needs; some of it to do with long-term use of the product concerned, so that its size and proportions become part of its brand image.

Proportions tend to give a feeling of balance and stability, as might be suggested by a heavy base, tapering toward the top, in the case of bottles as plastic containers.

Above: This label is beautifully crafted in a way that evokes traditional values in association with a natural product, but it has a clean sense of balance and proportion that is equally contemporary. The word "Brie" is nicely proportioned and letterspaced to fit within the circular frame just below center, anchoring the upper and lower elements of the design. Red and green are standard traditional colors, but the tonal and chromatic values of these particular hues are in line with modern preferences. They present sufficient contrast to read well against each other and stand out on the clear creamy background.

Above right: The color values applied to the lines of type on this bottle give them more or less equal weight, although the type sizes vary: the smaller type printed in white projects as strongly as the larger colored words. The proportion of lettering on a bottle has to be carefully considered, so that whole words are readable from a given viewpoint. In this example, the design also has to give prominence to the seal embossed on the glass; the approach to the typography is restrained.

COLOR VARIATIONS

How a color is perceived is determined by the colors that surround it, and partly by the size and proportion of the colors relative to each other. Differing proportions have been used here to show some of the effects that can be achieved as a result.

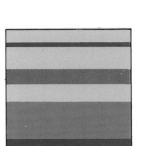

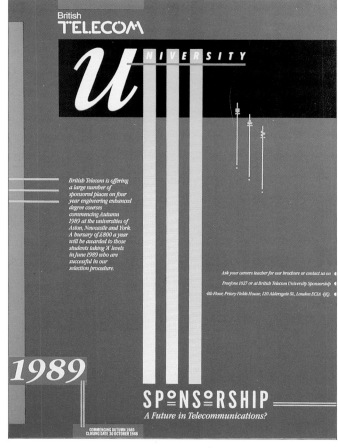

In modern design it is often the functional requirements of an internal structure that determine the outward appearance of a manufactured item. The adage "form follows function" is still applicable, so that the best and most elegant of modern design is characterized by a simple geometrical division of the design area, to give guidelines on which to hang the design elements of type, image, trademark, pattern, and color. The unity is created by the underlying grid framework, in which all the larger and smaller components of the design are related to the overall shape and size of the whole.

Although size and proportion are often determined by practical considerations of packaging, this can offer the designer a chance to concentrate on the purely visual as opposed to the structural element of the design. One glance at the rows of similarly sized cereal packets on a supermarket shelf, or a vast array of cigarette packs, shows how well or not the designer has managed to put over the product's image.

Above: The proportions of the colors are the first thing you notice about this purely abstract design. The large, light-toned yellow area is balanced by smaller sections of darker tone. The black type letterspaced across the yellow is highly legible.

Right: Vertical and horizontal stresses break up the format of this design without completely dividing it. Color is used for information and decoration: black, blue, and green locate the type areas while the red and yellow bands provide a formal contrast.

COLOR VARIATIONS

How a color is perceived is determined by the colors that surround it, and partly by the size and proportion of the colors relative to each other. Differing proportions have been used here to show some of the effects that can be achieved as a result.

MODERN

Pattern and Texture

Traditional images often bear the mark or imprint of the tool that crafted them. An obvious example is that of hand-drawn lettering and calligraphy, with the differences of Oriental script, the rounded Latin uncial, the angular Gothic black letter, and the elegantly engraved copperplate script of the European baroque period. Faded or sepia-toned inks, in combination with thick, yellowing paper, convey the impression of age and tradition.

Although many modern goods are created in plastic, recent innovations in technology allow the grain of wood or the texture of paper to be imprinted into the material. Other textures evoke the feel and appearance of woven, braided or knitted fabric, and the patterning may copy the centuries' old tartans of Scottish clans or the intricate geometric designs of Persian carpets.

Above: Colors associated with the natural colors of the product are used here in a contrast of patterned and plain areas. The pattern motifs sit on a subtly striped ground. The color vignette around the illustration is a traditional device, as is the outlined type with drop shadow.

COLOR VARIATIONS

Traditional patterns tend to be figurative and highly textured, often drawing on the pattern books of different eras for inspiration.

Right: Regular repeat designs suggest continuity, and with carefully selected motifs can promote an image of reliability and naturalness. In this design, which is reminiscent of old-fashioned wallpapers, the colors have a brightness that is distinctively modern and the color range has an upscale feel, thereby combining the best of both worlds. The impression of a well-established reputation is implicit in the choice of a copperplate-style script.

Modern patterning is typically orderly, simple, and geometrically regular. It exhibits a particular concern for the balanced integration of background and foreground elements of color and form, and this is often at its most adventurous when it seeks to create new forms for which there is no precedent, such as newly invented electronic products and equipment.

The development and widespread use of plastics meant that patterning and texture had become something of a lost art. Much of what we associate with modern design still tends to be smooth, untextured, functional, precise, and high-gloss. Where texture is considered appropriate, it is often when the "truth to the materials" rule is applied. Nowadays, however, the material is the message, and the true fabric of the material is allowed to reveal itself, rather than lie hidden behind layers of paint or decoration.

Left: The dominant character of these black and white patterns provides a brand image that is easy to identify. The labels are confined to allow the pattern areas to read strongly. In a market area where a range of color values is typically exploited, a confident monochrome statement can be an effective selling point.

Below: In this inventive calendar all of the information and imagery is color-coded to form a pattern in itself. Legibility and focus are provided by the variation of hues and tones, enabling the reader to identify the layers of information.

COLOR VARIATIONS

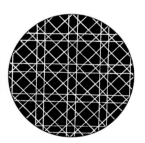

Modern patterning is usually geometric and regular with strong graphic shapes, while the texture is often smooth and glossy.

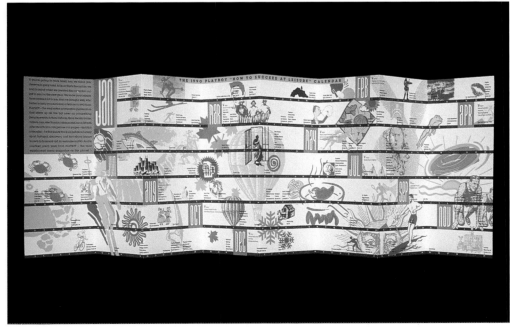

CLASSICAL

Classicism implies images that have stood the test of time, and have been shaped slowly and with more careful thought as to their balance, relevance, and purpose. The discipline of classical form is best emphasized by a limited palette of colors that is restrained and well-balanced.

The cooler, more passive colors – the blues and grays – and the monochromatic range from silver and white through gray to black seem to be more closely linked with the classical in our minds.

Form plays an important part, and simplicity of line is a prerequisite. Simple, geometric, elegant patterns in clear regular structure also evoke the classical.

plain
serious
rational
symmetrical
restrained
standardized
puritanical
discreet
poised

elaborate

whimsical

irrational

asymmetrical

unrestrained

exaggerated

passionate

unpredictable

cavalier

The romantic image is one of inspiration, adventure, and surprise, of emotion and feeling put before tradition and form. The warmer and brighter colors seem to sum up the warmth of romantic feelings and ideals, with pinks, purples, golds, and royal blues much in evidence.

Romantic imagery seems closely associated with texture – of rich and sensual silks, velvets and brocades, swirling patterns and sweeping gestures.

Romance in design can take several forms, and much depends on the context, whether it is the romance of adventure or encounter that is at its core. Bolder and brighter combinations and colors are more appropriate for the former, while gentler, pink and golden combinations seem to sum up the latter.

ROMANTIC

Color Associations

Over the centuries the concept of classicism has become associated with purity of form, unadulterated by the sensuality of color. To promote a feeling of the classical it helps to opt for simple monumental forms devoid of decoration, in which the natural materials can play a prominent part.

As far as colors are concerned, monochromatic or cool-colored schemes have a strong classical formality. The blending of tones like muted sea greens, silvery blue, and pale violet purples rather than the use of sharp contrasts encourages a feeling of gravity and restraint. Classical, laid-back imagery is well suited to the promotion of luxury goods, such as fine wines, expensive perfumes, and hand-made items, although any product which seeks to be taken seriously, from over-the-counter medications to corporate identities, may benefit from the classical idiom.

Right: The classical impact of this image comes from the carefully balanced and restrained use of color, coupled with simple abstract shapes. The design has an eternal feel to it, while being very much the product of recent design trends.

Below: Simplicity is also the keynote of this design, with a classical feel to the proportions of the white ground and colored band. The colors are directly representative of the stars and stripes motif. There are subtle touches of gold, a color that typically denotes a standard of excellence. The classical character of the design also stands out in the clean presentation of the serifed typeface and its centered layout.

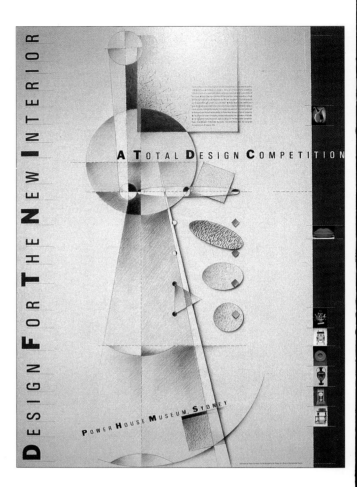

Right: Romance implies adventure and excitement, and the associations with it are being used to sell Turkish Delight. Here the rich pinks, purples and golds of the pack convey the impression of an Eastern seraglio, while the oriental-style typography and the strong image of the hand holding a cutlass creates the excitement.

The colors of romanticism are extravert, liberal, and light-hearted – the bright reds, yellows, and purples in the warmer section of the color wheel – while the forms are often bold and curvaceous, strongly reminiscent of the styles of the rococo and Art Nouveau periods.

Another side to romanticism, the dreamy as opposed to the adventurous, is evoked in the more subtly blended combinations of colors – the yellows of soft candlelight, the misty mauves and pinks of magical sunsets, and the rich deep reds of wine and roses.

Soft-focus photography and warm, blending colors can help create a mood of intimacy and dreaminess when promoting products with a romantic link – after-dinner drinks, lingerie, or cosmetics, for example.

Left: The romantic colors of sunset, golds, pinks, and mauvres – are often employed to create romantic-style images. Here, the actual sunset itself is used, the birds on the wires (forming the notes of a bar of music) silhouetted against the sky. The typography is, typically, curly and ornate.

Combinations of Hue

The dominant visual impressions called to mind by the classical are white, silver, and gray, symbolizing purity, combined with a simplicity of form. Subtle tints of cool greens such as pale sea green and lime green, and cool blues, such as aquamarine, ice blue, and lavender, are typical of classical restraint.

Harmony is the key word of classicism, and occurs when the quality and quantity of a selected number of colors are in perfect balance.

One of the most classic schemes is a monochromatic black and white, either in the simple form of black typography on a white ground, or in black and white patterns. A modern variation on a classical theme is the popularity of gray and white mixed together.

Optically, white or silver surfaces readily adopt the color cast of any light reflected from colored objects nearby. Combinations too harsh for the restrained classical idiom can be softened by adding a proportion of white to each.

Above: Over subtle dark and mid-toned gray marble patterns separated by white, the type changes from black on white to white on black where appropriate, so that it reads clearly. Small orange arrows provide flashes of color directing the eye to the written message. Classical imagery is directly utilized.

Below: A limited palette of colors, and particularly the gray reminiscent of engravings, give this packaging a classical feel, reinforced by the gold, roman serif typeface, and the fine gold rules.

COLOR VARIATIONS

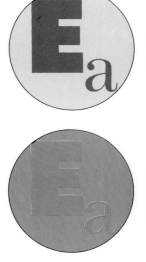

Monochromatic combinations or cool, pale tones are often used to create a classical atmosphere. Classical combinations imply: Permanence, solidity, strength.

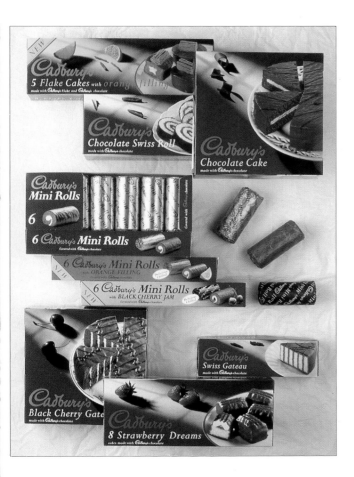

Left: The deep purple that is Cadbury's trademark color is cleverly blended with photographic images of the product by softening the image area into mauve and orange lights and making use of dense cast shadows. The unified impression of warm, rich hues suggests luxury and comfort, with high quality implied by the gold script of the brand name.

Below: The pastel palette applied to this product range has a sugary effect appropriate for candy. The sensual reds and purples are made gentler because light in tone, and complementary colors are brought into play. To give definition to the information on the pack, the type is consistently outlined with a darker, contrasting color.

The principal hues associated with Romanticism are the sensual reds, pinks, purples, and violets which can be contrasted with small quantities of lively apple and emerald greens, or cornflower and cobalt blues, in combination with deep, velvety blacks.

In general, the romantic impulse calls for an unrestrained and unfettered color palette, evoking feelings of *joie de vivre* and freedom of expression. Looking at large areas of red is known to generate physical excitement, since it is responsible for the release of adrenalin, which quickens the heartbeat.

The warm glow of polished gold is an apt choice, especially combined with rich, deep reds and regal purples. It evokes images of the Renaissance, of courtly love, and the intimacy of dinner for two.

COLOR VARIATIONS

Warm, vivid hues sometimes combined with toning, darker hues, create a romantic impression. Romantic combinations imply: Excitement, emotion, adventure.

Tone and Saturation

In classical art and design, color is usually subordinated to the molded sculptural forms expressed in highlight and shadow. The ordered tonal contrasts of classicism may be represented by the Doric columns of ancient Greece, the fluting catching the sunlight and creating both stark and subtle contrasts of light and dark.

The quiet discipline of classical order is best suggested using a limited palette, with variations of a single desaturated green or blue hue, graded regularly from light to dark. Any colors included would be restrained and well balanced. Pale cool colors are the most acceptable, the deeply saturated, vivid colors creating too brash or jarring a note.

Below: This design plays subtly on the austere classicism of a monochrome scheme, relying on controlled tonal gradations that give solid definition to the letterforms. A fine, red-brown box rule provides discreet contrast; its hue and tone are designed to complement, not compete with, the logo's neutral color value.

Above: On a background of classically toned ivory and cream, the cool, low-saturation green of the logo has a more restrained presence than would be the case if it were black on white; the tonal relationship of the black image on brown is similarly low key. Both color solutions suit the elegant styling of the type and motif.

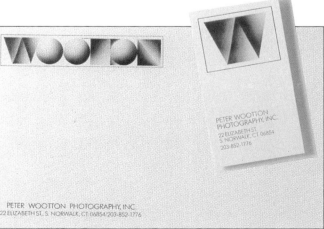

PETER WOOTTON PHOTOGRAPHY, INC.
22 ELIZABETH ST., S. NORWALK, CT 06854/203-852-1776

COLOR VARIATIONS

Dark tone   Mid tone   Light tone

Full saturation   Mid saturation   Low saturation

Top: Light to medium tones are more representative of classical language, with combinations that avoid sharp contrasts.

Above: Lowish saturations, often combined with mid tones, have the understatement associated with the classical.

ROMANTIC

Above: The mauve, pink, gray and gold color scheme, with curling scroll-like forms, together with the use of banners and gold leaf conveys a strong period feel and a romantic, almost Eastern impression. The use of the more saturated pink ground allows the lettering to stand out against a complex ground.

Romantic images aim to appeal to the heart and the passions, as well as the eye and the intellect. Soft-edged, warm colors can be held together in tender intimacy to create a dreamy romanticism. The more brilliant full saturations could be contrasted for a more dashing and adventurous romantic image. Worked into ornate patterns, separated by black, they recall Art Nouveau glassware with its richly jeweled colors in reds and oranges advancing from subtly blended backgrounds of pale green, blue, and violet.

Tonal contrasts that conjure up a feeling of "after dark," with lamp or candlelight casting shadows, evoke romance. Deep chestnut browns, and shadowy purples, highlighted with gold, can create an intimate atmosphere. On dark grounds, typography in gold will stand out while retaining a romantic feel.

Above: Strong hues and luxurious gold enhance the exotic imagery of these shopping bags. The background colors are unusually intense: purple offsets the image because it is dark in tone; the mid-toned red works well because of its dense saturation. Touches of vivid turquoise are an effective complementary contrast to the predominantly warm romantic colors.

COLOR VARIATIONS

Dark tone

Mid tone

Light tone

Full saturation

Mid saturation

Low saturation

Top: Contrasts of tone are often used in romantic combinations to create highlights and shadows.

Above: Saturations tend to be mid or full in the warm color range, often combined with deeper tones.

Shapes and Edges

Simple, geometric, straight-edged, and elegant forms are typically classical. Their structure is clear and regular. In classical architecture, the horizontal lintel, supported by vertical columns and capped by a triangular pediment, creates a satisfying balance, and the feeling of powerful forces at rest.

For any shape or design to be raised to the status of classical, it has to pass the test of time, implying that shorter-lived fashions have come and gone. Examples of classical forms that spring to mind are the Rolls Royce crest, the Doric column, and the champagne bottle.

The clean-cut chiseled forms of classicism reappear throughout the history of decorative art and architecture, and are borrowed and revitalized by succeeding generations of designers for modern application, including the latest advances in technology.

Right: A restrained and harmonious color scheme relying mainly on shades of gray needs distinctive edge qualities to create a three-dimensional effect.

This is achieved by careful application of shadows and highlighting lines, bringing out the individual forms in imagery designed on classical themes.

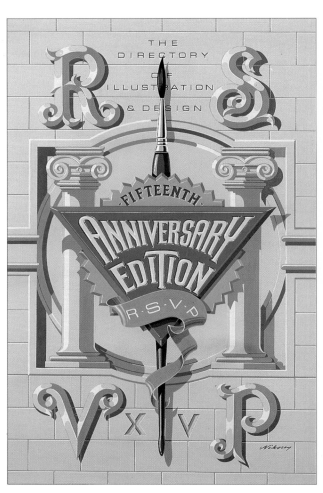

Above: A symmetrical framework gives a strong sense of balance, here represented by repetition of a roughly circular shape centered on the rectangular label. The hues applied to the images allude to natural colors, and the shapes are clean-cut because they are presented simply on a white ground. The label design is confined by a thick and thin black rule inside the edges of the rectangle, complementing black serifed type that is nicely spaced and proportioned.

COLOR VARIATIONS

The forms – the shapes and edges – that confine different colors affect our perception of them. The classical is suggested by:
- stable, balanced shapes
- clear, regular structures
- symmetrical design
- evenly spaced typography

Notions of the romantic are often best suited to the non-functional – in particular luxury products, impulse buying, and celebrations.

The typically romantic shapes are, of course, the heart and other organic forms, using curving and decorative motifs. Edges are rarely static, and seem sinuous, convoluted, and active, encouraging the eye to dance along with the spirit.

A rich historical source for romantically inspired shapes lies in the French rococo period of the early 18th century. The furnishings, decorative art, and design of this era are characterized by the bizarre, the flamboyant, and the richly ornamented.

Typography might be typically ornate and flowing, with curls, swirls, and ornate introductory capitals echoing medieval illuminated manuscripts.

Above: In this design there is a dreamlike quality to the imagery, which has a romantic flavor, described in the dense, rich tones of dark blue and red-brown. The contrast of color and tone allows the motifs to stand out clearly on the background, although they are soft-edged. The product label,

ultimately removed when the tissue box is opened, is boldly defined with hard edges and lighter tones to draw attention when it is on display.

Below: The collage technique applied to this design introduces a variety of shapes and edge qualities. The distribution of rich, romantic colors within a limited scheme of related hues helps to link them coherently. The representational images are both decorative and associative, suggesting gifts and celebrations.

COLOR VARIATIONS

The forms – the shapes and edges – that confine different colors affect our perception of them. The romantic is suggested by:
- flamboyant, ornate shapes
- rounded, curved forms
- italic serif typography
- decorated initial capitals

Size and Proportion

Classicism may be used to project an image which is morally uplifting or intellectually rather than physically stimulating. When applied successfully to promote the sale of one product over another, it can help to reassure customers that they are buying well-established manufactured goods of the highest quality.

Classicism is synonymous with the cool, dignified, and authoritative. In architecture it combines an imposing monumentality with nobility, strength, and generosity of dimension. In such well-proportioned design, every part has been considered.

In classical geometry great attention is given to ordered divisions of the whole. The most famous classical proportion is the golden section (thought to be ideal by Renaissance artists), which consists of dividing a rectangle in such a way that the smaller part is to the greater as the greater is to the whole.

Below left: A restrained and limited color scheme is applied to the labels of these wine bottles, with color coding denoting the type of wine. The design approach is unbusy, the labels unembellished; they are relatively large and a clean double rule marks the boundaries of a more typical size. The design is modern in character but its simplicity has a classic, timeless elegance.

Above: In a store display area designed in classical style, warm beiges and browns that refer to natural stone colors provide a restrained atmosphere for the decorative values of the products on show. Important features of the design are the marble and mosaic patterns and classic serifed type.

COLOR VARIATIONS

How a color is perceived is determined by the colors that surround it, and partly by the size and proportion of the colors relative to each other. Differing proportions have been used here to show some of the effects that can be achieved as a result.

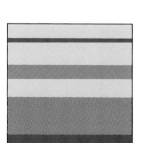 

Overall compositions repre-senting the romantic are typically unbalanced, asym-metrical, and irregular. The general feel of the romantic is of wholeness and balance, but one that is precarious and unstable, with the individual components of the design being inconsistent and eccentric.

The romantic image allows the designer considerable freedom to experiment with quirky com-binations of typefaces and un-likely combinations of colors coupled with a respect for human scale and proportion, so that the design is lively, energetic, and adventurous without alienating the viewer.

Above: The dark tones and unusual contrasts of rusts and sea-greens, coupled with the purplish background, evoke a strong feeling of mystery and adventure for this nursery rhyme-based imagery on a promotional biscuit tin for a design company. The text in the center stands out from the background tonally, yet is drawn into it by the continuation of the background image through the base of the box.

COLOR VARIATIONS

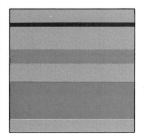

How a color is perceived is determined by the colors that surround it, and partly by the size and proportion of the colors relative to each other. Differing proportions have been used here to show some of the effects that can be achieved as a result.

Above: The contrast of the square shape of the plastic snopping bag with the diagonals of typography in cartoon shapes in vivid yellows, reds, green, and purples creates an exciting and adventurous image for a company specializing in licensed cartoon merchandise.

Pattern and Texture

In the main, classical patterning is dominated by the straight line and the perfectly poised relationship between horizontal and vertical, the most obvious example being the repeating fret or triglyph. The key words are order, symmetry, simplicity, and balance.

Classical texture is associated with the intrinsic patterning of the material itself – the veining of marble or the sculpted relief of the carved frieze, for example. Where color is relevant, and does not distract from the form, it usually consists of desaturated pale, dark, or grayed colors, confined within clear crisp boundaries and regular geometric patterns.

Right: Leather-effect binding and gold embossed lettering are combined on this book cover to create an upscale feel reliant on real texture, not a visual simulation. The deep burgundy color throws up the brilliance of the gold; the combination has traditional associations. The balance and symmetry of the design provide classical elegance, particularly the proportions of the type and image areas to the surrounding border – the typographic content is relatively compact and restrained for a book of this size.

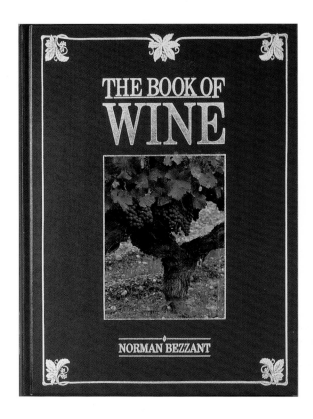

Above: These decorative covers for social stationery make use of frieze patterns bearing classical motifs from ancient civilizations, but the design approach is distinctively modern. The color themes relate to material textures associated with the historical references, such as crackle-glaze, marbling, and papyrus; these are reinterpreted with a contemporary feel in bright, appealing hues and tones.

Classical patterns are often smooth, architectural, and orderly, usually employed in a restrained manner in toning or matching colors.

Fanciful and florid, humorous, sensuous and vital are the images usually conjured up by romanticism. Having caught the viewer's attention with its quirkiness, it then encourages the eye to move across the entire surface, exploring its different textures and patterns. The romantic has none of the rigidity of the classical – it embodies the idea of flexibility, movement, and organic life. Many of the patterns are based on natural plant forms: entwining honeysuckles and columbines, lilies and orchids.

Romantic textures tend to look soft and yielding: the velvets, silks, and chiffons of fabric; soft, grainy paper in photographs with blurred, out-of-focus images; and the grain of rich, textured woods such as walnut, teak, and mahogany.

Romantic typography creates rich sweeps of curves and flourishes.

Above: Own-brand supermarket products are often typified by a fairly basic approach to design, but these tea packages are made deliberately distinctive and luxurious. The colors and textures in the photographic images are particularly rich and strong, and are enhanced by deep shadows. The eye is encouraged to explore the still-life elements in purely visual terms, but the objects also have nostalgic appeal. The images suggest a sense of privacy, luxury, and personal gratification.

Below: Floral motifs on the sides of these packs will create a repeat pattern in a multiple display, and the theme is emphasized by the larger image in the point-of-sale presentation. The colors are soft and pretty, relatively naturalistic, and they are displayed on a dark green ground that functions almost as a black in terms of creating contrast, but whose character is less hard.

COLOR VARIATIONS

Romantic patterns are flamboyant and detailed, in curling ribbons, scrolls, and banners, with a freedom of movement and expression.

RETROSPECTIVE

The term "retrospective" covers a wide range of styles and periods, but in design terms the interest focuses most commonly on the styles of Art Nouveau and Bauhaus, although the design icons of the 1950's and 60's are beginning to gain popularity as subjects for reworking in today's design idiom.

Each period has its own color associations from the greens, purples, and golds of Art Nouveau, through the blacks, grays, and whites of the Bauhaus, the abstract patterns in oranges, yellows, and browns of the 1950's, and the psychedelic colors of the hippie 60's.

The important element of any "retro"-inspired design is that it takes the best from the period in question and reworks it in a modern idiom, utilizing the advantages of improved modern printing processes to create exciting and inspiring designs.

saturnine

memorable

nostalgic

recollective

reminiscent

contemplative

melancholic

wistful

known

jovial

visionary

prospective

investigative

exploratory

projective

sanguine

courageous

unknown

The obvious sources of futuristic inspiration lie in the electronic age — space travel, computers, lasers, and microchip technology in general.

The colors associated with futuristic design are the bright jazzy reds, and greens of laser light beams, and their flickering patterns are an inspiration for the free form of much futuristic design.

The advent of computers has allowed designers a new freedom to create fanciful forms and objects in brilliant colors, whose shapes can be distorted, mirrored, textured, increased, or diminished at the touch of a button.

Modern synthetic materials and new methods of laminating give designers plenty of scope to experiment with form and texture, as well as color and pattern.

FUTURISTIC

Color Associations

The positive associations of a bygone age are useful for endorsing the lasting qualities of a brand name or product. For certain products, colors chosen a century ago still form part of the logo or label on a package or can. Though, for many people, the living and working conditions of the past had little to recommend them, it is to our notion of "the good old days" and the origin of the product in an age of greater craftwork or elegance that the continued use of such color choices appeals.

Many of the commercial names familiar to us today were equally familiar to our great-grandparents a century ago. Making the customer aware of this becomes a recommendation in itself that a product, such as a quality tea or confection, or the traditional design of a household product, has proved its worth time and time again. It is not uncommon for a well-established company proudly to incorporate its date of origin in its trademark or label.

Alternatively, a personal memory of color is associated with nostalgia, and recollections of youth or experiences of adventure and ambition, of unforgettable vacations, teenage romances, and the curiously outdated feel of popular color choices of the recent past.

Right: Associations with the past tend to invest a product with a standard of quality rarely achieved in mass production. The sculptural outlines, evocative colors and smooth shading used in depicting the food in this design for a supermarket chain recall the style of the 1940s and 1950s, suggesting the kind of service and quality associated with the old time neighborhood store, rather than the impersonal, off-the-shelf nature of modern marketing.

Left: This interior of a store in the Body Shop chain has capitalized on the period feel of its pharmacist's cabinet-style fittings to bring the idea of old-fashioned purity and excellence to its product. The period character of the display fittings, the company's logo, and the lettering on the product labels contrast with a clean, simple, and spare packaging concept that it is very modern.

To promote the future is to offer an exciting invitation to enter the unknown. Its positive associations are almost always bound up with the expectation of better things to come. To some extent, all advertising offers a promise of greater satisfaction once we have obtained what we desire. It is therefore to the optimism of the viewer that our designs must appeal.

Obvious general associations of the futuristic are with exploration, particularly space travel and the state-of-the-art electronics that has made space travel a reality. On the computer screen we are able to create vividly colored illusions and remarkably realistic visualizations of how new objects, forms of transportation, and future environments might look.

The "traditional" science fiction of the comic strip has also been overtaken by designers harnessing their imagination to the computer to generate fantastic objects and combinations of luminous colors, many of which have as yet no counterpart in the real world or on the printed page. The vision of the ultramodern is perhaps most associated with the luminescent helium reds and argon greens of laser light displays.

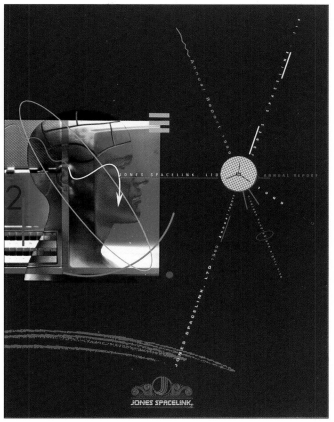

Above: A poster for an exhibition in France of Japanese graphic art incorporates a range of futuristic images and colors. The sharp and brilliant color contrasts, in shapes suggestive of sound waves and planets, clearly belong to the era of space technology and computer science. The shapes appear to float past against a dark void, with small dots like distant stars in the background.

Right: This poster design is very much in the vanguard of modern design trends, with its mixture of figurative and abstract images, laser light beam colors and asymmetric shapes giving it a surreal, almost ghostly quality. Although the printing is limited to two colors, it nevertheless creates a very colorful impression.

Combinations of Hue

It is a common figure of speech that we view the past through rose-tinted spectacles. The retrospective can encompass a wide range of color choice, extending from the vivid reds, yellows, greens, and blues of medieval coats of arms, manuscripts, and stained glass windows, to the popular wood engravings and harmonious color schemes of Arts and Crafts wallpapers, or even to memories of the shocking pinks and psychedelic colors of the 1960s and 1970s, with their characteristically garish fashions, automobiles, furnishings, and household consumables.

Other color choices which can be used to stress the retrospective include the sepia-toned photographs of World War I farewells and the tinted comic-book illustrations of the 1930s. Though full-color photographic reproduction was introduced over a century ago, it is only fairly recently that it has become commonplace and relatively inexpensive. It is therefore possible to evoke a feeling for the recent past by deliberately imitating alternative methods of color reproduction, such as hand-drawn lithographs, stenciling and *pochoir* techniques, and the hand-tinting of black-and-white photographs.

Right: This nostalgic pack design for Gitanes, the French cigarette company, is a masterpiece of its kind. Simply conceived, and even more simply printed, the cleverest element is the way that the typography stands out while being printed blue on blue, the color of contemplation and relaxation – states ostensibly induced by inhaling tobacco. The silhouetted dancing gypsy seems to move through the smoke.

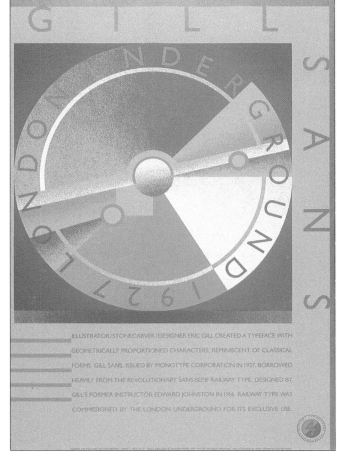

Right: One of a series of posters about the history of typography for Mercury Typography Inc. It celebrates the typeface designed by Eric Gill for the exclusive use of the London Underground in the 1920s. The cool clean blue, silvery gray, and gold design, smoothly airbrushed, successfully echoes the classic simplicity of the Gill Sans typeface.

COLOR VARIATIONS

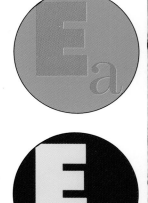

Associations with certain periods – vivid psychedelic colors of the 1960s, for example – create a retro feel. Retro combinations imply: Exclusivity, individuality.

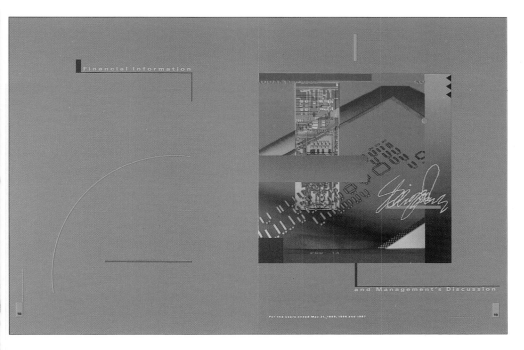

Above: This computer graphics poster, in which glowing flashes of color are set off by a neutral gray background, gives a virtuoso display of the new techniques now available to designers through micro chip technology. The computer has helped to create a new trend in graphic design.

Futuristic color combinations include most importantly the expansive and luminous yellows and oranges, traditionally symbolizing knowledge and the known, set against a dark blue or black ground, symbolic of the limitless or unbounded space of an unexplored universe. Typical "warm" yellows include primrose, saffron, cadmium, and amber, while appropriate blues include cobalt, gentian, cerulean, and indigo.

It is the usual function of a light source to lead the way, to light up new possibilities and illuminate the darkness. The ultramodern tends to be associated more with light sources than with the printed page, so that images of the future may be suggested by glowing discharge-tube reds, yellows, greens, and blues set against dark backgrounds or by the green-screen precision of the computer display unit.

While sunlight is the natural source of all colors in our environment, it is its luminous orange-yellow component that appears most outgoing and expansive. Orange-yellow is optimistic; it presses forward, toward the new and unexplored. At dusk the sun deepens in hue, before disappearing below the horizon to unlock the deep-blue vastness of the nighttime sky.

COLOR VARIATIONS

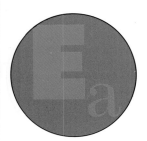

Vivid, acid, neon-light colors indicate a futuristic approach, often in strongly contrasting combinations. Futuristic combinations imply: Newness, difference, vitality.

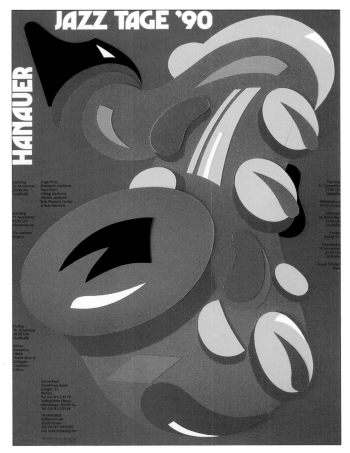

Left: This poster for Jazz Day '90 in Germany is an interesting mixture of the atmosphere of the 1930s' jazz club drawn into the imagery of the 1990s. The predominantly warm colors red, pinks, and yellows and rounded forms used for the semi-abstract saxophone shape, create a vibrant and lively image, while the sharp contrast between the red and green, and pink and blue, give it an "edge".

Tone and Saturation

In the academic art of the past, in which drawings were usually required to give a "sculptural" impression, great attention was given to the study of the modeling of objects in highlight and shadow. On completion of such a drawing it was often the case that repeated layers of delicate watercolor washes were painted over the completed tonal scheme to achieve the final, full-color effect. It may therefore be possible to suggest the past by imitating traditional approaches to painting and picture-making. The test of time might also be suggested when we attempt to reproduce the dark, varnished browns of Old Master paintings or the sun-bleached and faded natural dye-stuffs of old tapestries, fabrics, and wallpapers.

Long before ordered rows of fluorescent striplamps illuminated glaring, shadowless interiors, private houses, streets, and theaters were sparsely lit with inadequate, flickering flames. It has become popular in recent years to imply the coziness of such atmospheres in certain bars and restaurants, for which appropriate decorations and graphics have been devised.

Above: Much of the design of the late 1940s and early 1950s featured mid-toned, fairly low saturated colors that blend harmoniously in the design – possibly a reaction to the era of uncertainty that had preceded it in the war years. These designs for seed packages – a promotional giveaway – have something of the same feel, evoking the cigarette card designs that were prevalent in that period.

Above: This Canadian computer-generated design has embraced both the past and the future in its use of the sepia-tinted photograph, the calligraphy, and the lightly saturated background in similar tones, which are contrasted with the almost electric, highly saturated blue of the tinted image in the bottom right-hand corner. Owing to its saturation, this becomes as dominant as the larger background image.

COLOR VARIATIONS

Dark tone

Mid tone

Light tone

Full saturation

Mid saturation

Low saturation

Top: The degree of tone depends on the period that is being recalled. Light tones and brilliant colors for the 1950s; darker tones for Art Deco.

Above: The degree of saturation depends on the period being evoked – psychedelic 1960s colors being the fullest.

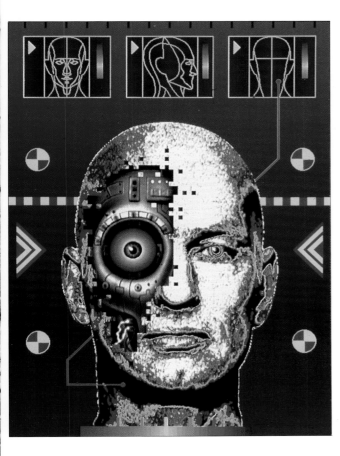

Most of us like to envisage the future as bright and optimistic, full of hope and expectation. Such an impression might be given by stark contrasts of tone, such as that provided by a bright light source spreading its rays across a darkened space. Under sunlit or fluorescent illumination, such an impression can be exaggerated by using luminous or Dayglo paints in combination with standard non-luminous colors. Particularly effective here are highly saturated yellows and orange-reds set against deeper blues, promoting a very different feel from the faded or earthy browns more reminiscent of the retrospective.

With so much in the urban environment clamoring for attention, technological developments can be used to create ever more eye-catching images. Fluorescent-panel advertising is now commonplace, together with banks of television screens used for advertising and entertainment in airports and shopping malls. The purest light available is obtained from laser devices which can be controlled with computer systems to create vast decorative, multicolored images.

Above: This obviously computer-generated design for Headline Books makes good use of strong contrasting hues to add richness and depth to the image, which draws heavily on the modern techniques of satellite mapping.

Right: This poster design, submitted for a competition, relies heavily on contrasts of tone to create a dramatic atmosphere in a surreal, almost desert landscape. The contrasts of tone are emphasized by the sculptural forms.

COLOR VARIATIONS

Dark tone   Mid tone   Light tone

Full saturation   Mid saturation   Low saturation

Top: Light to mid tones are best suited to the bright, acidic colors associated with futuristic effects.

Above: High saturations tend to create the brilliant neon-light impact of sharp futuristic colors in strong primaries.

Shapes and Edges

Other than adopting banners, ribbons, and medallions, a simple shape often used in connection with the retrospective, in company logos and advertising, is the ring or amulet, analogous to the figure of the serpent devouring its tail (an ancient symbol of eternity). In graphics and packaging it is often used to encircle a distant image of the past. Appropriate edges can be soft and out of focus or hand drawn, or involve the use of the dark or black contours commonly used to separate colors when printing registration was not as accurate as it is today.

To stress the positive qualities we like to associate with the past in newly introduced goods, it is not uncommon for designers to borrow and restyle images and decorative features from the graphics and decorative arts of recognizable past periods. Thankfully, the designer wishing to exploit nostalgic retrospection has an extremely rich source of shapes and patterns from which to choose. Over the last 100 years the Arts and Crafts, Art Nouveau, and Art Deco styles have each provided a particularly extensive and useful vocabulary of forms.

Left: A poster for an exhibition of 1950s' style at the Geffrye Museum in London captures exactly the main design elements of the period, with the rounded, cut-out, and moulded furniture shapes – introduced in the 1950s with the advent of mass-produced plastic materials – and the faintly "chemical" color palette (in this case, greens, red and creams). The overall pattern, in which no single element grabs the attention, was also typical of the period, and creates just the right "wallpaper" pattern for this poster.

Above: Printing directly onto tin was one of the big breakthroughs in advertising around the turn of the century. The package here is an essential element in the whole design, illustrating to what extent package shape and style has to be married to the overall design concept of the product. The round shape of the container (suggestive of the old ceramic pots) is emphasized by the swirling panels and the curving type, executed in *fin de siècle* style.

COLOR VARIATIONS

How a color is perceived is determined by the colors that surround it, and partly by the size and proportion of the colors relative to each other. Differing proportions have been used here to show some of the effects that can be achieved as a result.

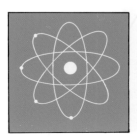

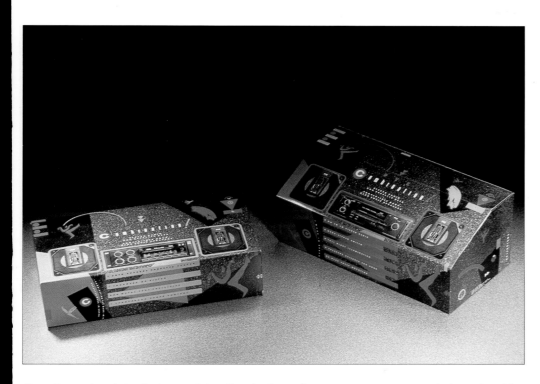

We need only examine the pages of science fiction magazines to discover popular notions of the futuristic, including other-worldly visions of eerily lit forms and creatures in strange unearthly yellows, purples, and violets.

In considering the realm of fantasy, the design tool that offers perhaps the most effective springboard into future possibilities is the computer. On the computer screen the most fanciful shapes and objects can be brought to life with remarkable realism. At the touch of a key, imaginary objects can be distorted, reshaped, mirrored, textured, made larger or smaller, fatter or thinner. The highly saturated colors (especially reds, greens, and blues) possible the computer screen combined with its characteristic qualities of pixel texture and edge can be used to imply the ultramodern.

Since many designs have not only to reflect current tastes but also to anticipate future trends, the computer now acts as a valuable design tool to construct, visualize, and examine possible new forms for containers.

Above: These package designs for Pye car radio/stereo cassette players exploits many of the features of modern design to put over the image of state-of-the-art technology, with its combination of photography and artwork, the textured background, small, brilliantly colored areas of type, and equal strips of color.

Below: This advertisement for a satellite television company uses overlapping images against brilliantly contrasted diagonals in oranges/red and green to give the impression of speed and split-second timing. The contrast of rectangles and diagonals creates a very active impression, while the imagery – of television screens, the globe, and sports – indicates the nature of the company's business.

COLOR VARIATIONS

How a color is perceived is determined by the colors that surround it, and partly by the size and proportion of the colors relative to each other. Differing proportions have been used here to show some of the effects that can be achieved as a result.

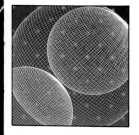

Size and Proportion

To sell an image of the past is to sell a tried and tested image. To consumers of modern, ephemeral, and mass-produced goods, the proportions of old objects appear well-crafted, generous, and attractive.

In referring to retrospective design, we only have to look to old books or museum showcases and catalogs to establish the traditional size and shape of objects from the past. In designing packaging and graphics for wines and whiskeys we may choose to emphasize their maturity. For reproduction furniture, traditional herbs and spices, crockery and ceramics, cookies and confections, it is not difficult to discover and revamp old-fashioned containers and labels of the appropriate proportions. Similarly we can exploit any number of distinctive typefaces, such as the serifed, shadowed, and outlined letterforms popular for handbills and posters a century ago but rarely used today except for circus and craft or country fair advertising. Early 20th century package design tended to exhibit flat, bright colors combined with bold, calligraphic letters, printed on uncolored card.

Right: The imagery of the 1930s has been borrowed for this theater poster for a revival of Noël Coward's work. The stylized figure has been created with sharply contrasting blocks of color in low saturations, the impact coming mainly from the contrast of jagged shapes and smooth flat areas of color. The asymmetrical central shape is pulled together by the repeated use of color – the pink of the words "Star Quality" and the background to the type on the upper right of the poster, and the blue of the number 5 and the diagonal shape of the rug. The pale mauve outlining of the image also has a 1930s feel.

Above: Drawing on 1950s comics' imagery, this poster puts the dynamic curved shapes of the car to good use in an arresting design. The strong, curved, red shapes advance against the flatly drawn pastel blue and beige background, and the dominating image is balanced by the boldness of the traditional black typography at the top and bottom of the poster.

COLOR VARIATIONS

How a color is perceived is determined by the colors that surround it, and partly by the size and proportion of the colors relative to each other. Differing proportions have been used here to show some of the effects that can be achieved as a result.

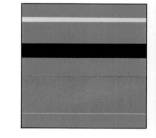

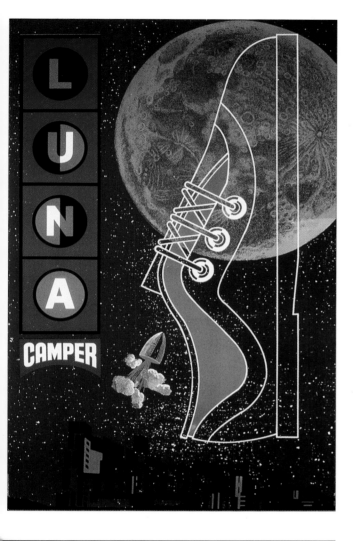

As with most graphics and visual imagery, it is a matter of size and proportion that determines whether or not a small-scale picture catches our attention sufficiently to appear representative of full-scale reality. A little over a century ago the painter's primacy in depicting the outward apperances of objects was usurped by the color photographer. In recent years, the computer screen has enabled the designer to explore future possibilities with such convincing realism that we may need little suspension of belief to be pesuaded that the experience is not real or within our grasp. In computer-aided graphics and design the proportions of both real and imaginary models can be extended, distended, or distorted at will, according to instructions programmed into the computer memory.

To a large extent, all concepts of the futuristic appear ridiculous in retrospect, though all have in common the belief that future environments and life-forms will relate to the human size and scale.

COLOR VARIATIONS

How a color is perceived is determined by the colors that surround it, and partly by the size and proportion of the colors relative to each other. Differing proportions have been used here to show some of the effects that can be achieved as a result.

Above left: One of a series of advertisements for Camper Luna shoes. The space imagery of the moon set in the galaxy, the upturned rocket shape of the shoe – echoed by the small rocket below – and the sun/moon effect of the reversed lettering in the word "Luna" have a coherent, forward-looking appeal.

Above: A poster design for an open-air opera in Switzerland relies on very simple contrasts of shape and size for its impact, the central globe cut by the highly saturated, light-toned crescent moon which attracts the eye first, even though it is small.

Pattern and Texture

In contrast to the stark and somewhat mechanical impression given by much modern design, the patterns, textures, and typefaces of earlier centuries often appear richly ornate and decorative. It is possible to call to mind the atmosphere of such periods by imitating past methods of patternmaking, such as woodblock printing, copperplate engraving, stenciling, weaving and stitching, and by imitating lacy or floral patterns, or meticulously realistic drawn or painted images. Laborious wood engravings were used extensively before photography be-

came widespread, so that imitations of 19th-century book illustrations immediately evoke a feeling of the past.

For many products, such as manufactured gift packaging in which the designer is permitted to give extra attention to detail or printing, the choice of more expensive materials, such as glass rather than plastic, or wood or tinplate rather than cardboard, can also succeed in promoting the desired effect.

Above: An advertisement for a banking house has used the homespun imagery of a 19th-century sampler to promote its tax deduction account. The cross-stitch-style lettering, the textured canvas-like background, and the soft coloring create a deliberately user-friendly approach, far removed from the glossy, hard-edged and abstract images normally used in financial advertising and promotional literature.

Left: This label design for Classico Pasta Sauce, one of several for different flavors, has deliberately evoked associations with the past and with nature to convey an image of the new sauces as traditionally good, wholesome, and of natural quality. The patterned border and strongly textured, wood-cut appearance of the illustration, create a warm cozy feeling suggestive of the best good home cooking.

Retrospective pattern draws its inspiration from different periods, such as the twining forms used in Art Nouveau.

Above: The inside pages of a brochure for a financial corporation has used an updated scrapbook approach to try to give a "cold" subject a more user-friendly appeal. The black-and-white striped background pattern, and the asymmetrical but carefully balanced shapes created by the pages help to give it a lively, fresh appeal. The vivid yellow flashes on each page have been positioned to give the design unity.

Below: A section divider introducing "Quality and Design" in the Next catalog for Spring/Summer 1991. Clearly the product of computer graphics, it mixes shape and pattern in an unmistakably modern way. The contrast of the purple and green is modified by the use of toning areas of black with white, and by the use of repeating shapes. The text and black strip form horizontal patterns thoughout the design.

While many designers, artists, and architects look to the past with respect and reverence, in the 20th century, advances in creative art have almost always been bound up with a desire to stand perpetually on the edge of the new, the stimulating, the challenging, and the unknown.

One factor which links the two extremes is that the rules established some 500 years ago for representing the structure and appearance of the visible world have proved to be an ideal means in contemporary computer-aided design with which to visualize with convincing realism what the future may have to offer. Virtually all textures apparent in the real world, including matte and glossy finishes, and the distinct tactile and visual qualities of metallic surfaces, are now convincingly reproduceable on the computer screen.

The Renaissance artists' perfection of the logic and geometry of strict linear perspective, the study of the relationship between light sources, highlights and shadows, and other graphical symbols used to depict depth, distance, solidity and texture, are all being utilized to depict remarkably persuasive images, sufficiently realistic, for example, to prepare astronauts to cope with imaginary tasks that no human being has yet experienced for real.

COLOR VARIATIONS

Futuristic patterns tend to echo the flashes and bleeps of the computer screen, usually in vivid fluorescent colors and asymmetric arrangements.

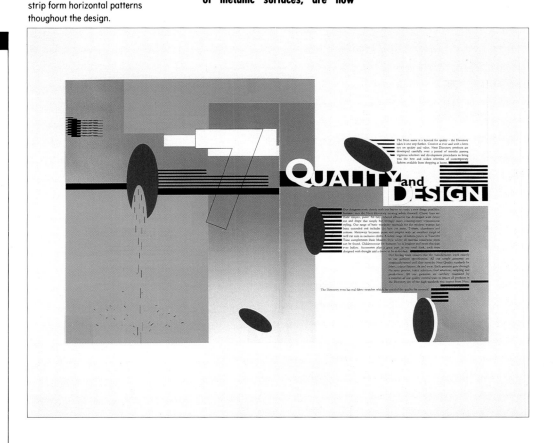

INDEX

Picture credits

Quarto would like to thank the following for their permission to reproduce the illustrations in this book. Every effort has been made to identify the copyright owners and we apologise for any unintended omissions.

6a	Sayles Graphic Design	60a	John Doyle, Eric Meola, Paul Silverman, Mullen/Wenheim	99c	Roundel Design Group
6b	Roundel Design Group	60b	Martin/Williams Advertising Incorporated	99b	McColl Group Ltd.
7a	Philippe Apeloig			102a	Paul Mullins
7b	Sayles Graphic Design	61a	Gestetner	102c	Paul Mullins
8a	Carter Wong Ltd	61b	Design Group Italia	102b	Michael Peters & Partners
8b	Design Board Behaeghel	62a	Bob Conge Design	103a	Cato Design Inc.
9a	Smith & Milton	62b	Lansdown Design	103b	Bossardt Design Limited
9b	Le Clan Design	63a	Rolando & Memelsdorff	104a	Michael Peters & Partners
10a	CS Coopstudio	63b	Blackburn's Limited	104b	The Ian Logan Design Company
10b	Sayles Graphic Design	64a	Designer: Barry Gillibrand, Michael Peters Limited	105a	Chrysalis Group plc
22a	Milford-van den Berg Design Wassenaar	64b	Elmwood Design Limited	105b	Matsuya Ginza
22b	Helmut Schmidt Design	65a	The Yellow Pencil Company	106a	Michael Peters Limited
23a	Rolando & Memelsdorff	65b	The Yellow Pencil Company	106b	Milford-van den Berg Design
24a	Pentagram Design Limited	66a	Design Group Italia	107a	Windi Winderlich Design-Kommunikation
24b	Michael Peters Limited	66b	Grace & Rothschild	107b	Design Group Italia
25a	Sanrio Company Limited	67a	Gibbs Design Incorporated	110a	Blackburn's Limited
25b	Cato Design Inc.	67b	RSCG Limited	110b	Cato Design Inc.
27a	Elmwood	68a	Thomas & Perkins Advertising and Tom Nikosey Design	111a	Vernal & Company Limited
27b	John Racilia Associates	68b	Ralph Colonna, Farrell Strategic Marketing Design	111b	Jim Allen Design Team
28a	Nettle Design Limited			112a	Pocknell & Company
28b	Zimmermann Asociados S.L.	69a	Tom Nikosey Design	112b	Walter Swartz Design Group Inc.
29a	Sidjakov, Berman, Gomez & Partners	69b	Tom Nikosey Design	113a	Pocknell & Company
29b	Bizart Packaging & Graphic Design	70a	Cato Design Inc.	113b	Gibbs Design Incorporated
38a	McRay Magleby, Brigham Young University	70b	Minale, Tattersfield & Partners	118a	Stan Everson
38b	Zimmermann Asociados S.L.	71a	Bossardt Design Limited	118b	Peterson & Blyth
39a	Seymour Chwast of the Pushpin Group	71b	Sayles Graphic Design	119a	The Jenkins Group
39b	Günther Kieser Visuelle Kommunikation	74tl	Siebel Mohr	119b	Seymour Chwast, The Pushpin Group, New York
		74tr	Alan Chan Design		
40a	Walter Swartz Design Group Inc.	75a	Smith & Milton	122a	Tom Nikosey Design
40b	Pocknell & Company	75b	Blackburn's Limited	122b	The Hively Agency
41a	The Yellow Pencil Company	75c	Smith & Milton	123a	Lansdown Design
41b	Minale, Tattersfield & Partners	77b	Yasuo Tanaka	123b	Design Group Italia
42a	Selame Design	78a	Lansdown Design	124a	McColl Group Ltd.
42b	Kazuaki Murai	78b	Akizuki	124b	Pentagram Design Limited
43a	Cato Design Inc.	79a	Michael Peters & Partners	125a	Alison Moritsugu, Julie Haynes, Mary Head, Phillips Design Group
43b	Walter Swartz Design Group Inc.	79b	Nettle Design Limited	125b	Robert P. Gersin Associates Inc.
46a	Gibbs Design Incorporated	80a	Design House Consultants Limited	126a	Quarto
46b	Design Board Behaeghel & Partners	80b	Rod Dyer Group	126b	The Partners (Design Consultants) Limited
47a	Design Board Behaeghel & Partners	81a	Michael Peters & Partners	127b	Michael Peters & Partners
47b	Minale, Tattersfield & Partners	81b	Quarto	131a	Kazumasa Nagar
48a	Shigeru Akizuki	82a	Tana & Co.	132b	Michael Mabry Design
48b	Cato Design Inc.	82b	Taylor & Browning Design Associates	133b	Günther Kieser Visuelle Kommunikation
49a	Cato Design Inc.	83a	Smith & Milton		
49c	Colourworks	83b	Gibbs Design Incorporated	134a	Walter Swartz Design Group
49b	Schmidlin & Partner	91a	Quarto	134b	Bossardt Design Limited
50a	Michael Peters Limited	91b	Mark Hess	135a	Headline Books plc
50b	Birth Defects Study Centre	94a	Walter Swartz Design Group Inc.	135b	Weymouth Design Incorporated
51a	The Duffy Design Group	94b	Rolando & Memelsdorff	136a	Nettle Design Limited
51b	Sayles Graphic Design	95a	Pentagram Design Limited	136b	Carter Wong Limited
52a	McColl Group Limited	95b	The Jenkins Group	137a	RSCG Conran Design Limited
52b	René Gruau	97a	Carter Wong Limited	137b	Bossardt Design Limited
53a	Giant Limited	97b	The Jenkins Group	140a	Paul Shupanitz, Tom Nikosey Design
53b	Minale, Tattersfield & Partners	98a	Estudio Hache	140b	The Duffy Design Group
56a	Alan Chan Design – Gianna	98b	Claude Kuhn-Klein, Switzerland	141a	Weymouth Design Inc.
57a	Sarah Cousin	99a	Roundel Design Group	141b	Sarah Cousin
57b	Pocknell & Company